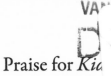

Praise for *Kids Who See Ghosts*

"*Kids Who See Ghosts* looks at the subject of kids seeing ghosts from every direction, bringing new and positive perspectives to a subject that has frightened people for generations. Finally, a responsible and realistic point of view!"
—Meg Blackburn Losey, Ph.D., author of *The Children of Now, Parenting the Children of Now,* and *The Secret History of Consciousness*

"*Kids Who See Ghosts* is a wonderful bridge between everyday life and the life of spirit. Author Caron Goode provides profound and useful tools for parents."
—Lynn Andrews, *New York Times* bestselling author of the Medicine Woman Series

"This is a much-needed book that opens the gates of communication and allows children to talk about their psychic experiences without fear of ridicule or judgment."
—Yvonne Perry, author of *More Than Meets the Eye: True Stories about Death, Dying, and Afterlife* and *The Sid Series: A Collection of Holistic Stories for Children*

"A fascinating compilation of science, theory, and intriguing personal accounts. Her compassionate heart guides parents confidently into the uncharted territory of the spirit world."
—Debra Snyder, Ph.D., author of *Intuitive Parenting: Listening to the Wisdom of Your Heart*

"*Kids Who See Ghosts* is a compelling resource that draws upon Goode's vast experience as a psychotherapist and provides a valuable tool for parents dealing with a paranormal concern."
—Jack Rourke, renowned psychic, parapsychological researcher, and author of *Ghost Talk*

"*Kids Who See Ghosts* can help parents with children who are sensitive to the unseen realm understand what their child is experiencing. It can also provide healing for adult children who came into contact with ghosts as a child by helping them discover that what they experienced all those years ago was indeed real."
—Rita Louise, Ph.D., author of *Dark Angels: An Insider's Guide To Ghosts, Spirits & Attached Entities* and host of Just Energy Radio

"Caron Goode reminds us that we as parents may not believe in disembodied spirits, but we always have the responsibility to empower our children by listening to them, taking their experiences seriously, guiding them to a sense of safety, and teaching them to trust their own perceptions and find healthy boundaries."
—Laura Markham, Ph.D., founding editor of *AhaParenting.com*

"Read this book and allow yourself to remember and celebrate all the unexplained experiences from your childhood that you eventually learned to forget."
—Lynn Serafinn, transformation coach and author of *The Garden of the Soul*

"Using fact-based stories from well-known psychics, as well as her own experiences, she helps the reader understand this special gift in children and shows why and how it should be fostered. I am a spiritualist medium and just wish my parents had this book when I was seeing ghosts."
—Glenn M. Smith, author of *Lotus Petal*

Kids

WHO SEE

Ghosts

How to Guide Them
Through Fear

CARON B. GOODE
EdD, NCC

WEISERBOOKS
San Francisco, CA / Newburyport, MA

First published in 2010 by Red Wheel/Weiser, LLC
With offices at:
500 Third Street, Suite 230
San Francisco, CA 94107
www.redwheelweiser.com

ISBN: 978-1-57863-472-9

Library of Congress Cataloging-in-Publication Data

Goode, Caron B.

Kids who see ghosts : how to guide them through fear / Caron Goode.

   p. cm.

Includes bibliographical references.

ISBN 978-1-57863-472-9 (alk. paper)

1. Children--Psychic ability. 2. Ghosts. I. Title.

BF1045.C45G66 2010

133.083--dc22

Cover and text design by Stewart A. Williams
Typeset in Garamond Premier Pro
Cover photograph © Jamie Carroll

Author photograph © Elusive Images by Laura and Grant (Laura McCarthy)
Printed in Canada
10 9 8 7 6 5 4 3 2 1

Contents

Acknowledgments

My thanks to the caring parents and readers of *Raising Intuitive Children* and *Nurture Your Child's Gift* for our continuing dialogue about parenting the future...our children and grandchildren. Let's continue cultivating our compassionate connections and conversations. Our network of heart energy supports everyone's mission and grace.

Many thanks and blessings to: Diana Bourgeois, who said to me after the launch of *intuitiveparenting.wordpress.com*, "You have a strong market here. These parents have questions that needs answers."; Tom Goode, my reader, loving best friend, and soul companion; Devra Ann Jacobs, agent and publicist, friend and guide, you are the best, and I feel it's an honor and a privilege to work with you; Jan and Red Wheel/Weiser for moving this book out into the world; and my deep appreciation to editor Amber Guetebier for her support, patience, and availability.

To the practical and gifted parents and professionals who gave me their time for storytelling, interviews, and editing to insure their clear messages, advice, and stories were clear and concise for readers.

Preface

*We see the world as we see it, and thus everything within
any person's viewpoint, is all part of the self-worldview of
that person.*

—CARON GOODE

"Mom, can I have my allowance?" I asked when I was eight years old.

"Sure. Here you are? What do you need it for?"

"I have to send it somewhere today."

"Wait a minute, Caron, not so fast. Where are you sending your money? Don't you want to put it in your savings account?"

"No!" I quickly stuck my one-dollar bill in a pre-addressed envelope and licked the seal. I was proud to be donating my money. The nun at school had provided the envelopes as a way to teach the children in her class to tithe. I knew nothing more of the envelope, only that she continued sending money for the remainder of that school year.

Sometimes, a visiting spirit, who looked like a bald, full-bearded man in a friar's robe, used to thank me for the dollar. He did not come often—perhaps two or three times in that school year. But I felt peaceful and happy when the spirit and his energy were around me.

Later, when I was a senior in high school, I noted that a Capuchin monk named Padre Pio, who had the stigmata during his adult life, died on September 22, 1968. An article about the Italian priest indicated that he could bilocate, or exist simultaneously in two places, and that he performed miracles of healing. In 2002, the Catholic Church canonized Padre Pio as a saint after years of documenting his miracles and bilocation. From his picture, I recognized him as the kindly spirit who had thanked me for my dollars. What a jolt to realize that I had seen a ghost, an apparition!

Or had I? Does a real human who can bilocate meet the criteria for being a ghost? Or can a ghost be only the spirit of a dead person? Or are ghosts figments of our vivid, fantasy-prone imaginations? Remembering my childhood conversations with spirit walkers opened doors to conversations with many parents and children about imaginary friends, ghosts, and relatives who had died and "visited." As a psychotherapist and coach for parents and children, I help families understand how a child might see a ghost and why it might be happening to them.

The Purpose of This Book

Kids Who See Ghosts takes an up-close and personal look at ghosts, the kids who see them, and the parents who want to help. The purpose of this book is to bridge the gap between the mainstream minds and the psychic minds, providing answers and guidance from eighteen parents; professionals in psychology, paranormal psychology, child development, near-death research, teaching, and shamanism; intuitive counselors and psychics; and a skeptic.

When children see ghosts, parents often wonder whether their children have a unique talent, need psychological help, or are experiencing a one time, weird event. Parental responses to their children's ghost sightings range from abject fear to supporting their child but being unable to act, to having their child visit doctors and therapists. The younger the child who sees a spirit, the more delicate the manner of handling such a situation needs to be, because the child's psyche is open and fragile. Many children and parents are afraid of ghosts, some to the point of physical illness. On the other hand, a whole different group of children are open and connected to the ghostly world and confidently, purposefully communicate with it.

From Blog to Book

I was excited to set up my first blog in winter of 2008 about intuition and working with intuitive kids in preparation for the release of my new book *Raising Intuitive Children*, coauthored with Tara Paterson. I'd spent months writing the book, yet coming up with my first blog entry of 250 words seemed especially difficult. Inspiration came in the form of a television program: *Psychic Kids* on the A&E channel. I watched it, was disappointed, and put my thoughts in the blog.

Viral marketing must have kicked in because the blog had tens of thousands of hits immediately. The audience was mostly parents asking for help with scared children whose bedrooms were full of ghosts, parents sharing positive experiences, and others asking "Is my kid psychic? Is she weird? Should he see a doctor? Does she need meds?" This book makes accessible not only my answers to parents' questions, but also *all* the information I received from and gave to others.

My motivation is simple. I cannot imagine a child, frozen in fear, unable to sleep in his own bed or refusing to enter her bedroom, growing into an adult who is not scared of their environment and world. It is time to talk about this stuff so that the next generation can be more empowered in the face of their fears and so that their parents might find understanding, reprieve, and compassion.

However, many people don't want to talk about kids who see ghosts for fear of ridicule. I approached one psychiatrist who said he would sue me if his name were associated in any way with ghosts. Another medical doctor said he couldn't speak publicly about such a topic, but spoke to me privately about his experiences. Like the elephant in the room, children who see ghosts exist, but we haven't conversed much about the topic.

Could Be in the Lineage

While interviewing moms, dads, and kids for this book, I also remembered my positive and negative childhood experiences with ghosts. I remember hiding under my covers from imagined ghosts in the closet until, drenched with sweat, I fell asleep. I remember being told to quit making up stories about seeing my grandpa, John, my mother's Irish father who died when she was young. Like other children, I thought all Catholics saw saints and that everyone's dead relatives, who weren't really dead, spoke with them.

Fortunately, not everyone in my family thought my experiences with Grandpa John's ghost were imaginary. My mother used to send me to stay weeks at a time each summer with Grandmother Ethel, her mother. Grandmother was deaf. When Grandmother spoke to me, she yelled. So our conversations were short, but highly relevant.

"Has John visited you?"

"Uh, yes, a man named John visited me, and he is the one in the picture you showed me. He was Mom's pop? Wow!"

As I grew older, we stopped talking about such topics. Grandmother never did know how much I appreciated those small but powerful conversations, because they validated some of my experiences. Grandmother's story presents two main keys to empowering children: listening to them and believing in them. You don't have to believe in ghosts, but believe in your child!

Opportunities for Empowerment

Seeing ghosts can be an opportunity for both children and parents to move through fear, explore different realities, and learn about the world of spirits. Ghosts can be children's best friends, and facing a fear of ghosts is a way for parents and kids to become empowered.

In the past ten years, the number kids who see ghosts has grown, as has the acceptance of intuitive gifts, like being psychic. And more and more kids are not shutting off their psychic perceptions after age six. What does the trend mean for the kids who see ghosts, as well as the rest of us?

My work as a transpersonal psychotherapist and spiritual coach and counselor has focused on four types of clients: (1) women, mostly moms, seeking spiritual support for chronic, severe health issues; (2) persons (adults and children) desiring to realize the self through their adversity; (3) persons who have had strange experiences, like dying in childbirth and returning to adjust to life, or sliding into an icy pond and being saved by a light until they could be rescued; and (4) children and their families who experience unusual phenomena and need a reality check.

What these types of experiences—seeing ghosts, facing death, touching the other side, and dealing with chronic illness—have in common is that they prompt people to choose between facing fears once and for all, or feeling and being helpless forever.

Helplessness breeds hopelessness and attempts to hide from life, which are really attempts to hide from fear while being fearful. Kids who are afraid of ghosts, just like children who deal with illnesses, need to face their fear to regain control of their environment. This book helps parents to empower themselves and their children, and enables both to regain control of their environment, whether it includes ghosts or not. For children who are shy and fearful of unknowns, this book provides myriad activities that will enable them to take small steps in order to gain confidence and grow into empowered persons.

Views Round the Rim

Ghosts and other such unknowns live within a metaphorical Pandora's box. This book opens that box to clear the air and breathe some new life into the topic for interested readers. Let's place the topic of kids who see ghosts in the middle of the circle and the various viewpoints about it around the outer rim.

As we read together, we'll move around the circle of viewpoints, so we can understand an expanded perspective of this hot topic. This book provides views from eighteen parents and professionals, a skeptic, psychics, and new-thought psychologists whose expertise and personal experiences shed light on seeing ghosts. In addition, the information for you includes discussions about making choices about ghosts, gaining control of environments, and children's ability to face fear and be empowered to take action when fear sets in. Life is to be enjoyed and for finding passionate purpose. If ghosts are part of that experience, then together let's explore why and how.

Dr. Caron Goode
July 15, 2009

Opening *the* Conversation

What Are Ghosts?

In *Beyond Shadow Worlds*, author Brad Steiger lists a variety of characters in the paranormal world, including:

1. Those who have passed over and are earthbound;

2. Spirits of nature, like fairies and elves;

3. Deiform spirits from ancient times who manifest around ruins (I call these spirits the keepers of ancient or holy spaces);

4. Spirit parasites, like demons and werewolves;

5. Spirit mimics that masquerade as ordinary people until their responses give them away or they are uncovered. (I am not familiar with and have not encountered these.)

Let's discuss these terms a moment so we have common definitions for this book. Most psychics and mediums interviewed for this book agreed that the majority of "ghosts" are the spirits of persons who have passed out of the body, but have not yet passed on to higher light or planes of consciousness. Those interviewed use the term *spirits,* feeling the term *ghosts* to be derogatory. Susan Gale, an intuitive teacher, uses the term *spirit walkers*—meaning those who walk in spirit, as opposed to those, like us, who still walk in bodies. For our purposes, we'll use the terms *spirits, spirit walkers,* and *ghosts* interchangeably.

Nature spirits, also called fairies, are beings that children see and interact with, especially in their preschool years. My grandmother once shared with me that she saw fairies in her luscious garden every year. She described them as tiny creatures with seemingly translucent wings. Two other children have described them in similar terms: "a blinking little light with wings" and "a teeny-tiny light the color of the flowers that moved around like they were flying."

Demons, werewolves, and other such parasitic entities also exist for some persons in spiritual or energy form. These entities are said to be conjured by human thoughts and fed by negative emotional energy.

In this book, ghosts, spirits, and spirit walkers are referred to as *apparitions. Apparition* means "appearing ghostlike" or "an unexpected image of a person." Angels, fairies, and others entities called guides can also be apparitions.

Where Is the Other Side?

> *The religious specialists of small societies—medicine people, shamans, priests, and priestesses—have, for thousands of years . . . taught a sacred body of knowledge . . . that opens a door to a reality separate from the ordinary world.*
>
> —BELINDA GORE

In this book, terms like *the other side, alternate reality,* and *beyond the veil* refer to the nonphysical world of spirit, as opposed to the world of more dense physical matter in which our bodies live. Spirit people walk in the spirit world or the alternate reality. People in physical bodies walk in the physical world.

In the interviews, you will find that psychics say the other side isn't like a place over the mountain and through the forest. Instead, the other side, as we discuss it in this book, is an alternate reality that permeates and exists alongside the physical reality. The light spectrum, as seen by the human eye, is a small slice of the continuum of light waves. We use terms like *other side* and *alternate reality* to refer to space that is different than that which our physical eyes see.

Mendizza Explains What Humans See

Michael Mendizza, author, educator, and founder of Touch the Future (*ttfuture.org*), which builds "bridges of understanding between the visionary research community and those who are caring for and mentoring children," clarifies what the physical eyes see:

> What do we think a "ghost" is? What does the term imply? Our interest in the notion of living and dying and the premise of ghosts involve the term embodiment—in a human body. It is interesting to consider that the embodied state is the only state. That is a very narrow definition.
>
> Generally we think of ghosts as not being embodied. A broader definition is to think of spirits or ghosts as patterns of energy along the vast electromagnetic spectrum of which we humans "see" but a small fraction, leaving most to what we call the unseen, which we usually dismiss as nonexistent.
>
> Most humans see a very narrow band of the electromagnetic spectrum—only the wavelengths of radiation between 380 and

760 nanometers—and we call this "light." On the other hand, a rattlesnake sees the whole infrared spectrum.

We know scientifically that the electromagnetic potential is not seen, yet it exists. We don't normally see those ranges. If we were sensitive enough to be able to dial into infrared ranges, like the rattlesnake is, we would see a very different world.

ELECTROMAGNETIC SPECTRUM

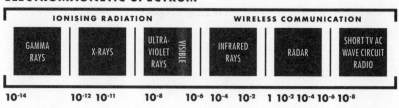

What the human eye can see, then, is a narrow range of the light spectrum; yet we define our world only by the light that our eyes perceive and our brain tells us we understand.

How Do We See and Understand Our Worldview?

Perception refers to how we receive information from the world around us and also how we process electrical signals. The perceptual process has several levels; in microseconds, the process

- screens information,

- chooses what aspects of that information to make conscious and what to delete as extraneous,

- fills in the blanks with data from our memory banks.

For example, the human eye sees only light, but the brain tells us we see so much more. We see the world in a specific way because our environment, cultural beliefs, and expectations teach us what things it is "normal" to perceive. We create a story that becomes our reality based on how our brains make sense of the light we see and organize it according to relationship and structures. In other words, we see what we expect to see. Remember, if the topic of kids who see ghosts is in the center of our discussion circle, then those who stand at the rim will view the topic based upon how they developed their perceptions.

Black Swans

> *Black Swan logic makes what you don't know far more*
> *relevant that what you do know.*
> —NASSIM NICHOLAS TALEB

In his book *The Black Swan*, author Nassim Nicholas Taleb opens with a story. In the Old World, people believed that all swans were white because they had seen large numbers of white swans. The discovery of the first Australian black swan, according to Taleb, invalidated millennia of fragile beliefs that all swans were white just because people had seen only white swans. Taleb names such events that invalidate widely held beliefs Black Swan events. Another example of a Black Swan event would be the attacks of 9/11, which invalidated Americans' belief that they were safe within the country's borders. Black Swan events are beyond our normal expectations, and they impact us significantly because they are unforeseen and shake us loose from locked-in perceptions.

Perhaps humans, especially children, seeing spirit walkers or spirits is a Black Swan, a seemingly random event. Or it could be part of an evolutionary growth of the human brain and consciousness. Or it could be part of certain people's natural talents finally being allowed to flourish in our households and society.

Are People Who See Ghosts Crazy?

Ghosts are a hot topic, as evidenced by the average ten million viewers of the television show *Ghost Whisperer*. According to a 2007 poll conducted by the Associated Press, 34 percent of people surveyed said they believed in ghosts, and those who believed included people of all religions and socioeconomic levels. Among this group are parents and grandparents who might say, "I took my kid to the doctor (or the therapist, or the priest), and they said he was fine—that nothing was wrong with him physically."

The questions being asked today by parents of children who see ghosts are these: Is something wrong with my child? Does my child have some sort of talent, like being psychic?

Psychologist Douglas C. Richards correlated subjective psychic experiences with dissociative experiences and confirmed that the former are common in nonclinical populations. From a psychological perspective, dissociation allows the mind to distance itself from experiences that are too much for the psyche to process at that time.[1] Dissociation is a normal defense mechanism and necessary for survival. It happens as a result of stress, trauma, or, as you will see later in the book, phase shifting or brain shifting. But not all dissociation is related to a serious mental health is-

---

1 Staci Haines, *Healing Sex: A Mind-Body Approach to Healing Sexual Trauma,* Felice Newman, ed. (New York: Cleis Press, 2007).

sue, like psychosis or schizophrenia. That means, as Richards writes, "Although psychic experiences are correlated with dissociation, they are not necessarily associated with pathology."[2]

So if you or your child sees a ghost, are you crazy? No! Younger children's brain waves linger in the dreamy states. Plus any person under stress or trauma can phase in and out of the brain states that are open to seeing apparitions. We'll continue to explore the question, are you crazy if you see ghosts, from different viewpoints. Even psychiatrist Carl Jung believed that ghosts and hauntings were universal occurrences. He thought that the scientific mind dismissed the subject too quickly.

From the Fringe to Convention

Authors Ryan Mathews and Watts Wacker, in their book *The Deviant's Advantage,* posit that changes in society drive changes in business. Every innovation starts at the Fringe, then moves to the Edge, then moves to the Realm of the Cool, then to the Next Big Thing, and finally to Social Convention. I believe that in current social terms, the phenomenon of children seeing ghosts has moved beyond the Realm of the Cool and is heading to Social Convention. Consider this cycle of moving from deviance to mainstream in relation to people's interest in gurus, meditation, alternative-health treatments, and energy medicine in the 1970s; today, these things are accepted by large numbers of people. Mathews and Wacker propose that what starts at the fringe of society usually reaches social convention within a twenty- to twenty-five-year period.

Another good example of a fringe interest that became a mainstream phenomenon is the public's fascination with extraterrestrials, which soared in the eighties. The movie *E.T.* made its debut in 1983, and Whitley Strieber's book *Communion* was a number one bestseller in the non-

---

2 Douglas C. Richards, "A study of the correlations between subjective psychic experiences and dissociative experiences," *Dissociation* (Vol. 4, No. 2), 83–91.

fiction category in the *New York Times* list for fifteen weeks in hardcover and for thirty-six weeks in paperback. *Communion* swept through the awareness of the masses, and some deep subconscious memories or archetypes were awakened in hundreds of thousands of people. They also remembered being visited by extraterrestrials. One Harvard psychiatrist, John Mack, M.D., brought credibility (depending upon your point of view) to the movement by forming a study group and writing a book recounting people's experiences with aliens.

Turning the page from the late twentieth century to the twenty-first century has brought the next big topic: *ghosts*. Television shows now feature tales of the psychic children who see or know ghosts and the adults who act as mediums for ghosts. The topic of ghosts is becoming the next big thing, and the realm of ghosts will soon become social convention. Watch out, expect the ghost wave to be as big as the extraterrestrial wave—perhaps more so.

Kids Who See Ghosts
and Their Parents

Creativity is the power to connect the seemingly unconnected.

—WILLIAM PLOMER

Children who see ghosts may see them not only in their childhood, but also in adulthood, even after they forget about their early ghost experiences. As a teacher, I worked with highly creative and imaginative children with special needs. My task then was to help them get through school by finding ways to help them learn and cope with the stress of what they faced each day. Whether in elementary, middle, or high school, most of the students were highly intuitive, and a few of them had what they called angels or guides to help them learn. I would never have known that these students' coping skills included a "wise friend" unless they had trusted me enough to tell me.

Two of my former students contacted me as adults, and we had further conversations of how my validation had given them hope and helped them learn. They explained that they had shut down their connections to their guides when they reached adulthood, but those doorways always popped open again, just like my perception reappeared during my Peruvian travels, as related in the following story about the monk who took the hot water.

The Monk Who Stole My Hot Shower

Weary, but enthusiastic, our little group of Americans arrived in the breathtaking city of Cuzco, Peru, mythical capital of the Incan empire and gateway to Machu Picchu. Less than a hundred years ago, Hiram Bingham discovered Machu Picchu hidden in the vastness of the Andes Mountains, at eight thousand feet above sea level. I was with a group who had come together to visit and learn more about this amazing place.

In Cuzco, which lies about fifty miles northwest of Machu Picchu, we arrived at a large courtyard off the main square and saw our hotel, a two-story, U-shaped building. The proprietor explained that this 350-year-old structure was once an elegant private residence owned by a Spanish lord and frequented by Vatican emissaries and Spanish nobleman. He led us to metal tables in the courtyard and served us *mate de coca* (coca tea), the local remedy for altitude sickness.

I craved warmth and rest due to the heatstroke I'd experienced at the "Candelabra of the Andes," the enormous geoglyph at Pisco Bay. I felt cold like ice since the heatstroke and having moved to different altitudes. Within the same week, our group visited the Nazca Desert and then journeyed higher in altitude to Cuzco. Our next leg of the journey would be Machu Picchu.

The courtyard of this old mansion was filled with colorful flowers that I didn't stop to enjoy. My mantra had become, "Hot shower, hot shower." I chose a large old key for a second-floor room; opened the room's heavy, carved door; and dropped all of my belongings on the bed. Then I stripped and ran to the broom-closet-sized shower stall to turn on the water. But only cold water drizzled from the showerhead; it wasn't even warm. For the next three hours, I spoke to the tour guide, the owner of the inn, and the patrons whose bathroom backed up to mine. I found no reason my room had no hot water.

Only when I was out of patience and near tears did the ghost who had haunted this room for the last 350 (so he said) years appear with a few answers. The room took on a cold, chilled air when a short, olive-skinned man stepped out from behind the red velvet drapery that covered the window. His eyes were penetrating, and his manner was intense, as if he were riddled with anxiety. He spoke Spanish, and I did not. Yet I understood him on an unspoken level. He sought help, and I saw in his mind the images of Spanish conquistadors beheading natives with long, curved swords.

Thank heavens, my roommate, Rosa, from Colombia, spoke Spanish fluently and offered to translate his story for me. Rosa sat on a wooden chair, and I stood behind her with my hands on her shoulders. We went into silence, inviting the ghost to communicate however he could.

The manner in which our communication took place was interesting because three levels occurred simultaneously in addition to the feelings of cold that we associated with the ghost. In the first level of telepathic communication, the ghost spoke Spanish to Rosa, who spoke to me in English. The second level was that I received the images the friar described in Spanish before Rosa translated in English to me. The third level was that Rosa was also receiving images, which she couldn't stop to describe and which we didn't need, as it turned out. Since the brain "speaks" by sending and receives images, unfiltered through Spanish or English, this form of communication makes perfect sense.

Rosa related that the friar knew he was dead, had died in the room hundreds of years previously, and was scared to move on because of his fear of going to hell, which had been ingrained in his thoughts from his life as a monk. He confessed that he was forced into a conspiracy to kill others and then started enjoying the act of killing. We never understood how many people he killed. When he was to return to Spain, he didn't go, but elected to stay in Peru in hopes of making amends for his horrendous sins. He had been haunted by his own fears and guilt for hundreds of years.

The friar's memories, as I viewed them, included the friar poisoning food and plunging a sword into a native. While I had no obvious way to confirm the information, Rosa and I validated the experience based on the similar images we'd seen.

The friar asked to be released from this space and helped to a place where he could move on. When I asked about the hot water, he indicated that he messed with it in order to get our attention, and he was successful. Indeed! When I asked if he would restore the hot water, he said yes. I called upon angels until we felt warmth and light fill the cold room. The friar also saw the light. He restored our hot water, walked into the light-filled area, and vanished.

After that, Rosa and I felt the room temperature returning to normal. And then, I went to stand for a long time under the steaming water.

LEARN FROM ALL EXPERIENCES

My former students related to me how they learned from their childhood guides. Even if initially frightened, they moved through their fears and arrived at acceptance so that any experiences with spirit walkers they had as adults brought further learning. I also learned something new from the experience with the friar.

When Rosa and I called upon angels to fill the room with light, which was a doorway that the friar used to move on, we felt completely "in the moment." Drawing from some inner experience or knowledge, I intuitively knew what action to take. I have used this image of a doorway of light in a dozen ways in my work with children and adults through the years. Some examples include:

- Eight-year-old Maria and I created a ritual for her to bury her hamster in her backyard, and she imagined that the hamster spirit scampered through a door of light after we buried the body.

- To calm anxiety in clients who are learning stress management or dealing with chronic illness, an easy technique is to envision this doorway of light, walk through it, and sit in the warmth and tenderness exuded by the light.

- In hospice work, when a client or friend is ready to pass over to the other side, the easiest way to prepare oneself is to imagine the doorway of light as a welcoming passage.

The following stories represent a variety of childhood ghost encounters that typify the range of experiences as well as parents' characteristic responses. You'll learn that professionals recommend that children who see ghosts have mentors to help them further develop their intuitive gifts. Often, children who see ghosts are called psychic, especially because of the abundance of media productions portraying people who communicate with ghosts. Thus come two questions that I am often asked:

Are all kids who see ghosts psychic?

Do all psychic kids see ghosts?

These questions are important to address because current television shows portray psychics as ghosts' helpers and television is a visual dimension, which children, especially in the age range of seven to twelve, often believe is real. These questions are answered in depth in *Raising Intuitive Children*. A summary of the answers follows:

- Brain mapping using EEG topography has found that creativity and intuition are associated with theta waves usually linked with daydreaming or fantasizing. Theta waves are calm states in which intellectual activity at the conscious level isn't occurring. Children and adults with ADHD produce excessive theta waves.

- Most people, children and adults alike, who see ghosts experience theta waves or brain-wave states of relaxation and meditation. People who practice psychic skills have learned to focus their attention or concentrate in those meditative states until it becomes as natural to them as practicing the piano is natural for a maestro.

- All kids who see ghosts are not psychic. Some children have a onetime ghost event. Many children experience brain-wave shifts for different reasons such as trauma, distress, fluctuating blood sugar levels, sleep deprivation, and even daydreaming.

- Children with intuitive learning styles learn through feeling, while others learn better through hearing or seeing. Some children who excel in this learning style have psychic capacities and abilities.

- Not all psychic children see ghosts—they may have a different gift than seeing. They might feel or hear a ghost rather than see one. Or they may have a combination of those skills.

Further along in this book, you'll discover that the professional psychics I interviewed felt they were born with that talent, have no fear of it, and work with both sides of the veil to bridge understanding and communication. Many people, not psychic themselves, have ghost encounters in their lifetimes. The most common is seeing a loved one after his or her death. The following stories present several viewpoints of children's ghost experiences and how parents responded.

Kathleen Dunham's Ghostly Playmate

Kathleen Dunham lives in Massachusetts and shares this ghost story that she remembers from age four. I include this story because it typifies what a child might imagine or encounter when left alone all day. Your children may relate similar experiences, and you might pay them no heed because you are busy like Kathy's mom was. Yet this child ghost was so real to Kathleen that she remembers him clearly forty years later. Was he a real ghost or an imaginary friend?

I am the youngest of four children, all of whom went to school during the day. Around age four, I was home with my mom, who was usually taking a nap, making the beds, or tending house. I had to keep myself occupied, and I watched television a lot. The next thing I knew, this little boy, around the age of ten, was there with me.

He was tall and thin with big ears. I thought he looked like Mickey Mouse. He came out from behind the chair and sat on the floor next to me. We'd play, or we'd get into mischief. I should say that *he* got into mischief.

If something in the house upset mother, she would say, "Why did you do this," and she would scold me. I told her honestly that I didn't do it. Then we would have circular conversations.

She'd say, "Who did it?"

"Peter did it."

"Who's Peter?"

"Peter the ghost. He lives behind the chair right there."

When Peter heard people coming, he would say, "Gotta go," and he'd get up and run behind the chair and kind of disappear into the floor.

Looking back, the experience was the weirdest thing. I would watch Peter come and go. When he left, I'd watch him go and then turn around and watch TV again. I wasn't afraid of him. He was like a playmate for about one and a half years. We moved from that house when I was around five and a half years old.

Susan Gale on Spirit Walkers

Susan Gale, coauthor of *Soulful Parenting*, offers transformational teachings through A Place of Light, tucked away in the hills and lakes in Cherry Valley, Massachusetts, southwest of Worcester. A Place of Light *(www.placeoflight.net)* is a center dedicated to supporting intuitive people and their families and friends, and it offers family camps, teleconferences, and yearly programs.

Gale was raised to believe she could do anything she put her mind to. Her father taught her to appreciate nature and understand people, and her mother taught her to keep her feet on the ground. She has always been a teacher in a variety of settings, including schools, camps, and child-care centers. She has trained many parents and professionals in ways of working with children through love and being positive.

While Dunham called her ghostly young friend Peter, and her mother called him "whodidit," Gale would have called him a spirit walker, based upon the Native American philosophy she believes in and brings to the people she serves through A Place of Light. Her philosophy embraces life in the physical and spiritual world as a continuum and is respectful of life in all forms. This philosophy provides an excellent framework for parents and children to understand and embrace spirit walkers.

SPIRIT PEOPLE

I call them spirit people. I believe that when the body passes . . . we all go back to the spirit world, since we come from the spirit world. There's really no change in who and what we are once the body is gone.

In this society, we don't do a very good job of teaching people about death, and so many people don't know they're dead when their body passes. Nothing changes, so it becomes a confusing time for them. When spirit people come across someone that can see them, hear them, or know they're there, they get very excited and tend to become very obnoxious, "Oh, you can see me!"

There are those [spirit people] who immediately go to the other side and don't hang around here, but many people don't realize their bodies are gone. People don't die, but their bodies do. So "ghosts" are people of spirit, as we are people with bodies.

I didn't see spirit people as a child, but my son did. One of my best experiences was when he was four. He came to me and said, "Momma, I just finished talking to the nicest man."

Since only two of us were in the house, I said, "Well, who was he? Tell me about him."

"I don't know his name, but he said to tell you he was sorry he didn't get to tell you goodbye."

I said, "Are you sure you don't know who he is?'"

"No, but I know where there's a picture of him." And my son showed me a picture of my father, who had died when I was thirteen. They had taken him to the hospital, he went into a coma, and I was never able to tell him goodbye.

That was a very moving experience. If I had told my son something like, "What do you mean you're talking to somebody else? There's nobody in here," look at the message I would have lost.

SOCCER MOMS AND PSYCHIC MOMS

We had one boy come to our school when it first opened. His mother was very excited because he could see spirits. He was showing me where he saw them in the room, and I said, "You really don't want to be bothered with this, do you?" When he said that he didn't, I let him know he had a choice: "You can just ask them to leave. When they come, you can just say that you are not interested."

That's what he chose to do, and his mother was so disappointed. But that was his right to choose. The spirits weren't his cup of tea at age nine. He learned he had a choice. Perhaps later he will choose that he wants to [communicate with them].

In the Native tradition, children are free spirits just like adults, so they have their rights, too. They shouldn't be forced to do things that they don't want to do. Some children love to see spirits, speak with them, and some children really don't. A lot of the parents try to live off their children, and they can't. We taught this boy's mom how she could use her abilities to see spirits herself, so she didn't have to live through her son to do it; she could let him be.

A Ghost Follows Lucy Home

This story about Lucy, a young girl whose mother contacted me after Lucy started talking to a ghost, demonstrates how stress can affect children's encounters with the spirit world. It also illustrates one common response parents have to their child's new spirit friend.

Lucy was eight when her parents divorced, which caused financial setbacks for her mother and father. Both of Lucy's parents lived in apartments, and she went back and forth between the two homes. Sleeping on her dad's couch when she visited him on weekends was her normal routine.

One night, Lucy woke up when she felt her favorite quilt being tugged. She opened her eyes and saw a young girl pulling the quilt off of her toes. Lucy wasn't frightened, only curious. She closed her eyes again, thinking she was dreaming and sleepy. If the girl were still there when she opened her eyes, she would be her friend. She opened her eyes and—voila!—the girl was still there.

The ghost returned with Lucy to her mom's apartment, and Lucy spoke with her friend, sometimes when she was alone in her room or sometimes before she slept at night. Lucy told her mom about her friend and said they had been conversing for about a year.

Did something bring the ghost to Lucy? Or did Lucy conjure up her new friend via her imagination, in response to the loneliness and stress she felt after her parents' divorce?

ARE STRESS AND SEEING GHOSTS RELATED?

Compare Lucy's experience with that of Kathleen Dunham, whose spirit playmate, Peter, disappeared when her family moved from the house. If Peter had been a product of Dunham's imagination, wouldn't he have moved with her? Peter's behavior suggests that his activity was independent of the young girl whose television watching was interrupted by a ghost.

On the other hand, Lucy was an eight-year-old single child of divorced parents. Despite the fact that she was slightly beyond the normal age range for having imaginary friends (ages two to six), she saw her friendly ghost at night, when she was in a sleepy state of mind. This is a good reason to say Lucy made up the ghost.

Also, Lucy had attracted a ghostlike figure that traveled with her from one parent's apartment to another. Moreover, the ghost became her confidante. As Lucy told her mom the ghost's story, she said the child ghost lost her parents to an accident of some sort. So Lucy and her friend shared a common loss. This could be another reason to say Lucy made up her ghost friend as a psychological crutch to get through her time of loss.

It is valid to say children may see ghosts because the children are feeling lonely or stressed. But did Lucy really make up her ghost friend?

MOM'S CONCERN AND MY RESPONSE

The conversation I had with Lucy's mom is one I commonly have with parents. The purpose of such a conversation is to help a parent discern their underlying worry, which may not be Lucy or the ghost, but a parent trying to deal with the divorce and financial setback.

"Should I take Lucy to a doctor?" her mom asked.

"Why?" I responded. "What are you looking for?"

"I want to know if anything is wrong with her."

"What if something is wrong with Lucy? Do you think a medical doctor can fix it?"

"I don't know. Maybe she is hallucinating and a drug would help her."

"Maybe and maybe not. From your mother's intuition, the part of you that knows your daughter, do you believe she has been hallucinating for a year?"

"No, not really. Lucy is really a bright student, well behaved, but I worry about her coping with this divorce."

"So you are saying that your daughter is still maintaining good grades and study habits, and the friendly ghost has you freaked out a little?"

"Yes, I want to make sure her dad and I haven't caused some irreparable damage."

"So this might be about you feeling guilty and not about Lucy having a ghostly friend?"

"Okay, maybe a bit of both."

Lucy's mom was worried that her actions during the divorce had caused her daughter to start conversations with a ghost, but I cautioned Mom not to transform her guilt into "something is wrong with Lucy, and I am taking her to a doctor for meds." I like to remind parents that children find their own ways to cope with life without medications and other ways of fixing what parents perceive to be wrong. Parents don't have to worry about fixing the children because the parents feel guilty that they might have caused their children to go off the deep end. Like adults who call upon inner resilience to get through stressful situations, children also respond to stressful situations in predictable ways.

I encourage parents to try to see the world from their children's point of view, because doing so may give them new insights into their children's behavior and coping strategies.

DISCERNING CHILDREN'S INNER DYNAMICS

I suggested that Lucy's parents keep weekly diaries of any behaviors that seemed unusual for Lucy—and changes in behavior that would warrant a visit to a psychiatrist. A month of consistently unusual behaviors could have caused the parents to visit a psychiatrist. When a child sees a ghost, you are looking for consistency in their study habits, grades, and social abilities, how they cope, emotional withdrawal, and outbursts. For example, did Lucy interact with the ghost consistently? Or did the ghost

---

Which Children See Ghosts?

Imagination is healthy and now recognized as part of the creative mind and intuitive intelligence. Surveys estimate that 65 percent of all children have imaginary friends during their first eight years of life. Surveys have also shown that these kids' communication and social skills develop faster than those of others. Two researchers in psychology at the University of Manchester in England found that the children in their small sample were more emotionally responsive, achievement oriented, and creative than other children. In fact, heightened creativity was a marked feature of the children in this study.[3] (If Lucy's mom had read this study, she might not have even questioned Lucy's friendly ghost.)

---

3 Douglas C. Richards, "A study of the correlations between subjective psychic experiences and dissociative experiences," *Dissociation* (Vol. 4, No. 2), 83–91.

happen to show up at specific times or after distressing events? Did Lucy seem aware and cogent, or were her thoughts inconsistent?

Watching for consistency in a child's behaviors and observing how he or she interacts with the world allows parents to understand the child's perception of reality, to see through the child's eyes. According to psychologist Carl Rogers, every person—in this case, a child—exists in a continually changing world, and the person sees him- or herself as the center of that world. One way to see what the world looks like from your child's point of view is to be with your child and consciously connect and listen instead of doing something to him or her, like Lucy's mom wanted to explore.

Being Person-Centered

Rogers formulated a specific therapeutic process, person-centered therapy, that focuses on a way of being with a person. As a parent, being person-centered with your child is not directing the conversation or solving the problem immediately. Rather, allow some time for catching your breath and connecting though a hug, holding hands, facing eye-to-eye so you are fully focused on your child. Next, being person-centered means listening without interruption and asking a few clarifying questions. A stroke of clarity is marvelous to behold when all the bottled-up thoughts have tumbled out and your child sighs with relief.

Don't assume anything when perceptions of spirit walkers are involved. Check what you understand with your child. Find out when it happens consistently, where your child feels fear most, and what ideas they have. Person-centered listening with respect tells your child that you do value them and you have faith in them. Your respect and positive regard is absolutely empowering.

Using that process of being with your child allows you to be aware of how he or she relates to the world and discover how to walk them through fears. Why does *being with* a child work? First, because you come with no preconceived notions or judgments; you are just exploring how a child experiences the current environment. Second, you don't look at what you think is wrong; rather, you observe what is working or seems to be not working. Third, you don't fix or pry; rather, you listen to the child's story and gain insight as to how he or she thinks and copes.

Since Lucy wasn't exhibiting any symptoms except seeing a ghost (over the course of a month, neither parent reported Lucy doing anything really unusual or abnormal, except that she seemed quieter than usual), I asked Mom to delay her desire to take Lucy to a doctor and give Lucy time. Maybe talking to the ghost was Lucy's way of coping with loss.

Based upon our continued conversations, Lucy's mom learned to be with and listen to Lucy with no preconceived judgments. She listened while they walked the dog or shared sandwiches at the park. She monitored the time Lucy spent alone in her room. She learned how Lucy was meeting her needs in coping with a divorce and loss of her family. With her mother's consistent presence, Lucy finally talked about saying goodbye to her ghost friend, in hopes the ghost would reunite with its own parents, wherever they might be. Lucy and the ghost had conversed for about a year.

Doreen Fisher and Her Children

Doreen Fisher is the founder and CEO of Rainbow Outsourcing in Plano, Texas, and the mom of two intuitive children who see ghosts. In her family, ghosts, fairies, and protective animals are the norm. By accepting her children's talents and connections to the nonphysical world, Fisher has taught her children to be confident. Like all children, they get frightened, yet they ask for help to negotiate with the ghosts and pets of the unseen world. Fisher's approach to child rearing involves bringing her heart wisdom to the forefront of the situations her family faces. She has developed a lifestyle of trust with her children by adapting to their self-worldviews, being willing to face her fears, calling for a friend's help, and empowering her daughter to sleep with ghosts in the room.

I asked for permission to include her stories because I feel her heart-centered acceptance and way of communicating with her kids about the topics of unseen spirits give all of us clear direction.

> *Nothing is impossible to a valiant heart.*
>
> —JEANNE D'ALBRET

INTUITION RUNS IN FAMILIES

Family members always called me super-sensitive. Empathy was definitely something that I tapped into, and I still do. Coming from a broken, alcoholic family was disturbing to me, because I always assumed that they were angry with me. Because of my empathy, I felt everything my mother felt, and I would take it on. She was troubled and in abusive relationships and very much in her head. She would get preoccupied, and I would feel the rise in her anxiety and stress levels. I would know it was coming before she would blow up. I knew to get out of the way.

I learned to listen to and trust my intuition, and to listen and trust myself with my children. I wanted my children's home environment to be different from my childhood's toxic environment of anger and shouting. I often wanted to hide. I found consolation when I picked up the flute, and I lost myself in music. I would play for hours and realized that it was my passion and my way to cope.

I found Dr. Christiane Northrup's book *Women's Bodies, Women's Wisdom* when I was twenty-eight. The message of the book to me was "I was born perfect. The rest is just beliefs that I picked up." For example, I had been tested over a period of twenty years, told that I couldn't have children, and successfully believed it. As soon as I read that book, I said, "I don't believe that anymore. I choose to believe that I am perfect and whole." I went off all these medications I was on to monitor my hormone imbalance, and three months later, I became pregnant with my first child, Mila.

OLD PATTERNS CREEP IN WHEN ADULTS HAVE CHILDREN

Isn't it the truth that our children are our greatest teachers? When Mila was ten months old, and I was nursing her, she popped up, looked at the ceiling, and got a big smile on her face. She waved and tracked something up in the ceiling.

I had chills over my whole body. I said, "Don't hurt her. Just don't hurt her." I was terrified of an unseen thing. I felt the presence. It may have brought up something that I had been scared of as a child, but Mila was smiling. This happened repeatedly, and Mila wasn't speaking yet.

When she was about two and sleeping in her own bed, she woke up in the morning and screamed at the top of her lungs for me to come in to her. I got frustrated because I'm like, "Just walk in here. Come to me."

When I went to her, the look of total fear on her face set me back. The fear was so real that she could not get out of that bed. She told me there were people in her room. I said, "There's nobody in here, baby, look." My response was habitual.

My nagging feeling kept saying listen to her. People tried to give me advice like, "Oh, kids at that age are manipulative. They'll just do whatever to get you to do what they want." My instincts said that's not true. I didn't buy it, and so I looked for other ways to help Mila feel safe when she saw people in her room.

A friend of mine suggested weaving a web of protection, so I told Mila, "Okay, I'm going to weave a web of protection around you." I visualized this light circling her body and crisscrossing until it was like a little cocoon of light all around her. She told me she felt safe and was able to fall asleep. I also felt Mila was now safe and able to sleep myself.

INTUITION GUIDES STONE'S HEALING

My son, Stone, was born with a heart defect, a condition called supraventricular tachycardia (SVT). It was like an extra electrode in his heart that would jump up to three hundred beats a minute and get stuck. I started having trouble nursing and was getting signs that something was wrong. The doctors and midwife said he was fine. Only because my gut screamed, "No, we've got to get it checked out," did we get to the doctor at the right moment because his heart was starting to fail. It was swollen, and the doctors didn't know the issue until fifteen hours later.

When Stone was two weeks old, the doctors told me he might die. At that moment, everything stopped around me and became surreal. An internal voice said, "That isn't true. Don't listen to that and focus on what you want." The doctor continued explaining the different levels Stone's health might take—possible heart transplant, death, being on medication throughout his entire life. One other possibility, that he might outgrow it, was the option that I chose. I looked at my son in the hospital, and I kept telling him that his heart was confused. Stone looked me directly in the eyes, and I knew that he understood what I was saying. "Tell your heart to heal, Stone. It knows how to do it."

The hospital staff laughed at me. I kicked the doctors out of the ICU and focused on surrounding Stone in positive energy. What happened next? The doctors said they didn't know why his heart healed. "He's obviously not reading the medical journals. He's healing rapidly, and we really don't understand why." They released him, and we went home to the rental we lived in.

A PRESENCE IN THE HOUSE

Back home, I was weaving webs of protection around Stone. I felt like a dark presence was in our rental and trying to take Stone away from me. That was the first time I ever saw a ghost. I was sitting in the living room, and I caught movement out of the corner of my eye. When I turned my head towards the door, I saw what I thought was Mila going to the bathroom in a pink nightgown. I waited a few seconds for her to come out, and she didn't. Something was wrong. I went in the bathroom, got instant chills, but found it empty. Mila was sound asleep in her bed, and she wasn't wearing a pink nightgown.

Once, when my husband, Mila, and I were on the couch, we heard a baby on the baby monitor. Since I was nursing Stone, all of us looked at the monitor and then at each other with wide eyes. We heard a baby crying on the monitor, but I was holding Stone. We went into the bedroom, and the monitor was unplugged. We still don't know what happened, and I still felt a dark presence trying to take Stone away. Whether it was true or not, I don't know, but that was the feeling I had.

At that point, Mila started hearing heavy breathing when she slept in the room with Stone. I would put them in my bed when she came to me and said, "I can't go to sleep. There is somebody in my room. I hear them. They are breathing really fast." Mila imitated the breathing pattern as panting sounds. That lasted for years until we moved again, and she seemed to be free of the panting ghost.

OTHER REALITIES ARE REAL

As soon as Stone could talk, he told me long stories about his animal friends. They all had names, and he could describe in detail how they looked. There were a lot of them. He had them around him all the time; but one consistent companion, called Tiger, was around him all the time. He called Tiger his protector, the one who always helped him. If he started to fall, he felt that Tiger was there to stop him.

At that point in motherhood, I wasn't sure of the state of these different realities. While I had let go of my fear, my son was interacting with real presences, not unlike children in other cultures who have power animals for their protection. By the time Stone was born, I had accepted the fact that Mila and Stone could see presences in other realities, and I could feel them.

MILA AND THE FAIRIES

At age three, Mila told me she saw fairies. When she was eight, she talked to her friends about it. They said, "There is no such thing."

She's like, "Yeah, you don't know. You just don't look for them." One friend asked her what they looked like, and she said, "They are little balls of light, and they are different colors."

"Oh, everybody sees them," one little girl replied. Mila's pragmatic response was, "Then everybody sees fairies." She never deviated from her story or her reality. I think it's because I support her that she trusts herself [and trusts] that it's true for her.

I have said to her, "You stay true to your heart, and people are going to tell you all kinds of things in life—even me, because I am bringing in my parents and their parents and their grandparents into my parenting. Only listen to the things that you know to be true."

SOME PRESENCES SCARE MILA

When Mila was seven, she slept in an upper bunk. When I came into the room, I saw her slammed up against the outside edge. I moved her to the middle of the bed. Yet every time I checked on her, she was squeezed to the edge again, whereas her usual sleeping pattern was very open and sprawled out. Mila spoke openly about the spirits she saw, but now the spirits were getting more intense. Se we dove deeper.

"What spirits do you see?"

"I don't know, but they are scaring me, Mom."

"Where are they, Mila?"

"They are in my bed, and there are more and more of them. They keep coming. And there is not enough room on my bed to fit any more."

"Can you tell them to go away?"

"I have, and they go away and come back."

So we cleared away the energies. We asked them to leave; they would come back and back again. We even took the mattresses off the bed, took them outside, and burned the sage around them. We asked the energies to leave, and they kept coming back.

Out of desperation, I said to Mila, "Okay, do you know that you are more powerful than they are?" She looked at me and was kind of confused by that. I said, "Do they have negative energy, or do they have positive?"

"Kind of negative. They're not very happy."

"Well," I said, "Are you?"

"Yes."

"I see you as just loving life. Is that how you see yourself?"

"Yes."

"I believe that how you see yourself is stronger than any negative energy, Mila. So you are stronger than they are, and you can let them go and tell them they can leave."

Suddenly, Mila had this realization that she was bigger than the energies were, that she could tell them to leave. Then she explained, "I just feel safer when you are here."

"I get that, I do," I said. "Understand that when I am in the next room, we are still connected. You and I have a very strong connection, and we are always going to be connected. So all you have to do is visualize that ribbon that connects us." We talked about what that ribbon looked and felt like. I said, "If you feel alone, just take that ribbon from your heart and snake it down the hallway as it dances. And it snakes around, and it dances as it goes, and it connects right to my heart. So you are never alone. And that ribbon can go all the way across the planet, you know, so it's just here."

Mila understood and started sleeping through the night after that. At some point, she started to have problems again, and I asked, "Do you think it would make a difference if you moved to the bottom bunk?"

"Oh yeah, they aren't down there. They hang out up here."

Stone chimed in, "Well, I can sleep up there, because Tiger will protect me. He won't let them hurt me." So they switched beds, and it was like instant relief.

Donna Seebo's Advice for Parents

Donna Seebo is an internationally acclaimed psychic, counselor, teacher, speaker, award-winning author, and host of a daily radio program, *The Donna Seebo Show*, on BBS Station 1 *(www.BBSRadio.com)*, an Internet talk radio network. She lives in the shadow of Mt. Rainier in the Pacific

Northwest, where her home offers a quiet retreat from her busy traveling schedule and professional responsibilities.

Seebo grew up in a family where spirits were recognized as authentic, and because of her childhood experiences and interests, she long ago learned to accept the world of the paranormal as commonplace. In June of 1977 she was ordained as a Spiritualist minister in Southern California. Like me, she feels that children need acceptance of their realities in order to help them not be fearful. Here are her thoughts on her personal experiences:

> When I started into the study of the mind, the psychic self, it was because of someone else who recognized my talents. It was my mentor, Gloria, who changed my direction of thinking and action so many years ago. It is so important for parents and individuals to know how significant that recognition of a child's intuitive talent is. I have interviewed many people through the years, and those who don't make fun of a child's perceptions can be quite amazed at children's clear and insightful observations.

ACCEPT CHILDREN'S REALITIES

> I am a Spiritualist minister. For ten years I worked as an assistant pastor in the First United Spiritualist Church in Gardena, California. Reverend Humble, the minister who passed away many years ago, had a tremendous love for children. He welcomed them into classes that their parents attended. He would frequently say, "With children, do not hide anything regarding experiences with spirits, because they will tell you the different things that they go through. Don't make fun of what they see. Don't worry about a child being frightened or harmed, because it's not going to happen that way. If you are fearful, the children will be fearful. If you are comfortable with seeing spirits, then they will be comfortable."

Reverend Humble's words were part of my introduction into the world of spirit communication and becoming comfortable with the whole environment of change that came with it.

When a child is seeing spirits and hasn't had anyone explain what is going on, it usually is not a frightening experience. However, if the adults around the child have a fearful attitude, then the child intuitively picks that up and adopts the attitudes of fear because he or she thinks that is what they should do. Fear usually evolves because one doesn't understand what is going on.

What we don't understand, we feel a repulsion towards. Why? Our survival instincts that automatically kick in warn us of potential dangers. This is natural. But we also have lots of false belief systems that others have taught us creating confusion as well.

What can you do if your child is seeing or hearing ghosts? Be willing to put your own fears aside and listen. Be willing to ask questions, to explore the subject matter, and to be curious enough to make notes and investigate what the possibilities might be.

"IT'S THE WORK OF THE DEVIL": CREATING OUR OWN FEAR

I'm going to sidetrack my comments for a moment to mention something that happened in one of my classes on psychic development. I was teaching my students how to use tools like the Ouija board, tarot cards, the pendulum, and other items as a point of focused concentration to tap into their intuitive talents. One student, a woman, spoke up loudly and harshly saying, "Oh, that is the work of the devil! The Ouija board is the most awful thing anybody could ever use."

My response was, "Well, that's fascinating to me. Can you tell me why the Ouija board is so terrible?"

She proceeded to tell her story. "It was during World War II. [The Ouija board was really hot stuff during that period as so many people were concerned about their loved ones being overseas.] My brother was stationed in Europe. My girlfriend and I sat down to work the Ouija board, and it just worked beautifully. This one day I sat down with my girlfriend, and after we put our fingertips on the planchette, it began to move very quickly. A message started spelling itself out, and to our amazement it was about my brother. I was shocked. The message said that he had been wounded, was in a hospital, and would be coming home in a few weeks. That was the work of the devil!"

Before I could say more than "That's interesting," she continued. "That's not all of the story. We got a telegram two days later saying that my brother had been wounded and was in the hospital. Later that same month, my brother came home. I put that Ouija board away in a closet and never again played with it. I just knew it was the work of the devil!"

This well-read, well-educated woman was sharing her very personal story with me and the class. She felt safe talking with all of us about an experience that she had categorized as bad so many years before. I thought her experience was a wonderful one. She obviously was a medium and didn't know it. The Ouija board was the instrument for her mediumship to come forward. The information had been quite accurate. Why in the world, I wondered, was she in my class? Was she trying to find some answers and be at peace with this side of herself? I determined that she needed some help in understanding what had happened so many years before.

So I said, "The Ouija board is only made out of paper. Take a good look at mine. It is made out of compressed paper. There is printing put on that paper. You can make one out of a tree stump, you can make it on a sidewalk, you can make it on any kind of surface or material you desire. The Ouija board is inert.

What gives it the energy are the people using it. You were the telepathic receiver, the conduit for this information."

We had quite a nice discussion regarding her experience, and when finished, she understood what really took place, and her whole attitude shifted from fear to confidence and understanding.

This woman created a fearful attitude that stayed with her for years because of lack of understanding. This is an example for all adults that I would like to address. Children don't have the blocks of discriminating attitudes that adults frequently develop. Adults will create fear where there shouldn't be any. Yes, we do create fears. Sometimes they are formed into superstitions and can be passed along for generations before being seen for what they truly are. We, as adults, create them. When we adopt the attitudes of our culture, society, religious beliefs— whatever we have been taught without questioning the premise or viewpoint—we get stuck with them. Too often we don't think through why we have the responses we do.

Fearful or superstitious thinking occurs throughout the world, within all kinds of environments, regardless of educational background. As adults, we should examine our thinking and not convey our fears onto our young children, as our children will mirror us all too well.

—DONNA SEEBO

PSYCHIC CHILDREN NEED MENTORS

As a counselor, minister, and teacher, Seebo plays a much larger role than that of a psychic, and she has assisted many people in her talks and writing. Her personal experiences shed light on the importance of mentoring psychic children.

Let me share some of my experiences as I was growing up as an intuitive child. Dreams have been an intimate part of my mind experience. I recall having vivid dreams that came true. Many times I was aware of flying or falling [in my dreams], being out of control of what was happening to me. I didn't discuss it with my family at all because it just wasn't to be discussed. Dreams were frivolous things not to be taken seriously.

During my teen years, I did learn that my grandmother was known as an exceptional healer whose power with prayer had saved an uncle's life and affected the well-being of many others. This wasn't discussed much either, as Grandmother was a religious extremist in the minds of some family members. I just kept to myself each unique happening that I went through.

My dreams were so real, graphic. Many, as I mentioned, were prophetic, and I considered them nightmares because I didn't know how to interpret them. There was one occasion where, during my dream, I hid in a closet and was awakened by my father when he opened the closet door. Apparently I had been screaming in fear and was unaware of what I was doing when I'd hid in the closet. The dream stayed with me, as it was a warning of what was to come.

A year later, my whole life changed in an unpleasant way, and the danger I'd perceived in my dream actually happened. But at that moment, I couldn't even open my mouth to share anything about my nightmare. Who would have even listened?

As adults, we need to be aware of ourselves and our perceptions. To understand our children, we must deal with our own prejudices. I encourage everyone to read about research on the mind. Be observant of recent publications and even old ones relating to the intuitive area of understanding. Be open and receptive to your own intuitive nature and continue to expand your own knowledge and education. Learning is a lifelong project, and we need to be good examples for the younger generation.

Children can be vulnerable because they don't have the experiences and the years of wisdom you have acquired. When you are young, you travel your particular path, which will bring many learning processes. Part of that journey is the development of your intuitive self. The right kind of support is helpful, and it shouldn't be encased in fear. We can teach children:

• To have the awareness of what is happening in a moment

• To have the self-confidence that enables one to be safe

• To have the freedom to talk about experiences and not be made fun of

• To find mentors one can trust and respect

Children today will resonate with someone that is real, and then they will be able to be more accepting of who they are. And it's so important. But education is the key, and having a mentor is so important.

SEEBO'S CHILDHOOD MENTOR

One of my favorite people and my mentor was my aunt, Juanita, who was only nine years older than I. I loved her dearly. One particular evening when I was visiting with her, she sat down with me at her kitchen table and talked about some profound moments in her life.

When Juanita was in her early teens, she and her sister decided they would go up to an old house on a hill in an area of

Virginia. This was a Victorian-styled house, and a "witch" who lived there told people's fortunes. Juanita's sister went in first, and then Juanita went into the room. She didn't know what to expect and wasn't sure whether she should be scared or not.

The truth was she was curious and sat down at the table, waiting to find out what would come next. This woman told Juanita that she hadn't been able to tell her sister very much, but she could read Juanita like a book. She told my aunt that she would meet a young man with an unusual walk. He would be in the navy, and the woman saw him going to sea. His walk was so different that Juanita would be able to spot him in a crowd of a million people. She would have seven children.

At the time Juanita wasn't dating anyone, but she met my uncle within a year. And he did have a very unique way of walking that distinguished him in a crowd. Also, Juanita had seven children, but only four survived, as three were miscarriages.

That same evening she sat with me in her kitchen, Juanita related an experience that saved her life. She had been going through a deep depression. Suddenly the room she was in became filled with a bright light. Someone talked to her, telling her not to give up hope and that she was not alone. There was a family Bible on a nearby table, and as she opened it, Juanita said that the pages became filled with the same bright light, which wrapped her in a warm cocoon of love. She felt this experience saved her life, as she had been contemplating suicide. I knew that Juanita hadn't shared this story with many people, and I felt so privileged to have her share her personal happenings with me.

You may notice that the stories Seebo shares illustrate several family factors. Intuition seemed to run in her family, and how children experience seeing ghosts or paranormal activity depends upon how others around them perceive the events—children take their cues from adults.

Her stories also indicate the importance of having a mentor, so children's perceptions of events "outside the box" don't have to be filed away as irrelevant or held as family secrets like Ginger's experiences were.

GINGER'S STORY: DON'T WAIT UNTIL YOU'RE SEVENTY TO ENJOY GHOSTS

What you can learn from Ginger's story is how *not* to handle your child's ability to see ghosts, or colors around people, or even predict a person's passing over. We don't want our children to keep secrets or be frightened of disclosing information about their talent. How can we parent them to be exceptional and lead meaningful lives with their ability to see spirits? Seebo continues with Ginger's story.

When I was in my twenties, green, and new to this field, a seventy-year-old woman came to me and said, "I want you to tell me why I've gone through certain experiences." When I think of her today, her story still amazes me, as I was to be her validation for all of her memories as a psychic child. Maybe Ginger's story will spark your own memories.

When Ginger was about four years of age, an "auntie" came to her house to visit with her mother. When the auntie was leaving, she gave Ginger a big hug, and the child smelled sweet, wonderful flowers. Then she saw brightly colored flowers all around her auntie. Ginger closed the door, and turned to her mom and said, "Mommy, Auntie's not going to be with us in two weeks."

Her mother got furious, slapped her, and said, "Don't you ever do that." Ginger was being punished for seeing the absolutely beautiful.

Auntie died a couple of days later. So this infuriated the mother. She didn't want Ginger to have her psychic awareness.

Obviously the relationship between the mother and daughter throughout Ginger's growing years was very poor.

Ginger realized, as she got older, that she could see lights around people—color frequencies of others' auras. Moreover, when she saw and smelled this fabulous bouquet of flowers, she knew a person was going to be passing on within a very short period of time.

As the mature woman who came to see me, Ginger was going through a very difficult period. Emotionally she was a mess. Her mother had come to live with her. She told me about another experience: "I got up, and I was all disheveled. I was in this ugly, sloppy robe. I walked downstairs, and my mother is at the kitchen sink, and I sit down. I heard a loud pop, and I was up at the top of the ceiling, looking down at myself. And I thought, 'God, you're ugly.' I could hear my mother's conversation. I could hear my daughter's conversation."

Ginger's mother turned around and looked at her, while Ginger, out of her body, watched. Her mother recognized something was seriously wrong and called the doctor. They lived out in the country, and the physician would come to see them. The doctor said, "I'll be there as quickly as I can. Walk her upstairs and get her into bed. By the time you do that, I will probably be at the house."

Ginger told me that she watched her mother frantically call for Ginger's daughter to come in, tell her, "Something is seriously wrong with your mother, and even though she's so heavy, we've got to get her upstairs into bed." The doctor arrived, walked into Ginger's room, examined her, and then took her right hand.

Ginger said, "I'm watching everything—quite content. I had no desire to go back into that body. But he started digging his fingernails into the palm of my right hand, and I could feel the pain. He kept digging and digging. He was starting to cause blood to come through the broken skin. All of a sudden—*boom*—I was back in my body, and I yelled out from the pain."

The doctor looked Ginger straight in the eyes and said, "Don't you ever do that again." He knew she was out of her body. He saw it. Ginger had never known such peace and joy as she did while floating on the ceiling.

Ginger didn't connect the dots, but I did. Ginger's mother knew what Ginger was doing and had gotten mental communication from Ginger. Her mother knew about all of this stuff and was in a state of denial about it. This was a talent that ran in the family. Ginger's mom also had experienced multidimensional time warps.

When Ginger finished her story, she looked me in the eye and asked, "Why me? This is horrible. I have been cursed."

I said, "You have not been cursed, Ginger, but you certainly haven't had anyone to talk about this to in your entire life." Ginger was very lonely.

Like Seebo, I have had parents, and especially grandmothers, share their experiences of seeing ghosts and angels or having out-of-body experiences. At trade shows, several grandmoms have explained that they could never talk about these experiences in their families. They bought my book, *Raising Intuitive Children*, to pass on to other family members. One man, a dad named Eric who was given the book by a friend, remembered his ghost experience after his son refused to sleep in a bedroom with a spirit walker. He shared his story for this book.

Kendall Helps Eric Address the Ghosts of Childhood

The story of Eric and his son, Kendall, illustrates another reason why parents might dismiss their children's experiences. If your child sees ghosts, you might remember your own frightening experiences and not want to revisit those memories!

Eric is a widowed dad raising his five-year-old son, Kendall. Life was pretty good for them until the night that Kendall refused to go to bed or even enter his bedroom. He reported that a man was in his room. Despite Eric's best efforts to search for the spirit and reassure his son that no one was there, Kendall not only pointed to where the man still was, but also described the spirit walker in detail. Kendall seemed unusually anxious about the man. Eric didn't ask his son much about the man, as he was more interested in making sure nothing was wrong with Kendall.

Kendall slept with Eric that night, and every night thereafter for a week, refusing to be in his bedroom. The family doctor found that Kendall had no symptoms of physical illness. Then a child psychologist pointedly asked Eric, "Do you believe your son?"

The question was an affront at first. Eric was indignant that anyone would question his support for his son. Yet the more he thought about it, Eric realized he didn't really believe Kendall saw anything. Eric chalked the experience up to Kendall's imagination and was more concerned with Kendall's fears and odd behavior.

As the therapist probed deeper, Eric remembered an incident from his own childhood when his dad, a coal miner, moved the family to a small town in West Virginia. The small home the family bought was said to be haunted, but Eric's dad dismissed it as nonsense, as did his mother and brother. Eric wasn't so sure. At age seven, he knew he felt chills every time he went to the basement to work on his model cars. The whole place was creepy, and one afternoon before supper, Eric saw a pale figure pass through the room. Terrified, he ran upstairs to tell his mother. Both parents heard and dismissed his story all in one breath. Embarrassed and feeling stupid, Eric pushed the memory deep inside for the next two years that his family lived in the home, but he had become shy of his environment and always felt like he was looking over his shoulder. He didn't want Kendall to be that way.

The psychologist explained to Eric that his own memory of an event similar to Kendall's was causing him to overreact to Kendall's anxiety about the man in his room. He asked Eric to sit down and listen to Kendall, not dismiss him, before continuing to take him to more specialists. It wasn't important that Eric believe Kendall's story about a ghost, but it was important that he give his son the time and attention and try to see through Kendall's eyes what was happening in *his* world.

Brad Steiger's Lifetime of Ghostly Experiences

The quest for absolute proof or completely objective truth may always be unattainable when it seeks to limit our souls.

—Brad Steiger

A true pioneer in the field of parapsychology and psi research is Brad Steiger, the author of over 170 books on paranormal topics. Because of his extensive investigations and personal experience with ghosts, psychics, and paranormal phenomena, I asked Steiger to share his stories and experiences with ghosts and spirits, some of which are also covered in depth in his most recent book, *Beyond Shadow World*. Steiger shared the reality of spirit walkers with his sister. Were they both psychic? Or does the fact that when they went to bed at night they saw the same ghosts of the old stagecoach prove that these independent entities live in a reality that is just outside the normal range of human vision?

For Brad Steiger and his sister, spirit walkers were simply part of their daily lives. Like a lot of children, Brad believed all spirits were basically good—until one adult experience made him change his mind. He supports parents and kids listening to their instincts and getting help if they do not feel comfortable with what he calls "astral masqueraders."

56

Having had such ghost experiences as a child, and after rising to prominence as a paranormal investigator and author, Steiger believes an evolution of consciousness is happening now. I asked Steiger to share his ideas about why more children are seeing ghosts and how he teaches parents to deal with spirits. He voices the questions of three generations and says that the answers to these questions lie within each of our worldviews.

You mentioned today that on the topics of ghosts and spirit walkers, many people believe that these entities are automatically good, or they might all be angels or a very wise grandfather who has passed on and comes back in wisdom. I try always to warn about astral masqueraders, as I call them.

Astral masqueraders—I use the term because my many years of experience have shown that we have to continually test the spirits. Here's why: The motion picture *The Sixth Sense* came out, and we all saw the young boy, Cole (Haley Joel Osment), going, "I see dead people." I was astonished at the number of e-mails I received from parents saying, "I want my child to be able to see dead people." They thought it was cool that this little boy was seeing dead people. I say I will not in any way participate in such forced development.

Now, if your child is normally and naturally seeing these entities, then be patient. Don't encourage, but listen to him or her. Don't ridicule, don't mock. Listen. He truly may be having mystical or psychic paranormal experiences, but don't force the child, because the astral masqueraders would love to come in. It's the same thing with teenagers and their Ouija boards. I tell them, leave those things alone. And do you know now that a Ouija board for children is available at Toys R Us? Truly.

CHILDHOOD EXPERIENCES

People often ask me how they can train themselves to contact spirits. I have never tried to contact spirits. They have always contacted me. I have never worked to develop mediumship. I don't know what it is in my psychological, chemical, or ancestral makeup that combined in my psyche, but I started seeing entities when I was just a child.

My sister and I shared similar experiences. Our home was built on the site of the old stagecoach stop, and according to local legend, that's where Jesse James and the boys stopped on the way up for the great Northfield, Minnesota, bank raid. The stagecoach stop had been torn down, and our home was built on the original site.

It was common for us to hear the sound of horses coming down the lane and to hear night noises. My sister and I are both insomniacs today, and we joke that it's because we kept being awakened all night long by the strange people in our bedrooms. We'd fall asleep after one visitation, and then there would be someone else bending over and staring at us. We would finally fall asleep, and then someone else would walk through the room. Sometimes they would not pay any attention to us. The interesting thing, more often than not, is that we made eye contact with the spirits at times.

My sister and I saw solid people, wearing essentially formal clothing. Men's styles really haven't changed since the Civil War, but the women were wearing clothes that did not seem contemporary to the 1940s when I was growing up. After a time, all of this became normal for my sister and me.

So I grew up feeling that spirit or ghost phenomena are just a normal part of life. We lived out in the country, and I did not see or play with other children other than my sister, who is four years younger than I, until I went to school. I had no way of knowing that this wasn't what happened to everyone at night.

In other words, in my world, my evening scenario started when night fell. We went to bed, and then people started walking around in the room. There was nothing to tell me otherwise. Of course, as one progresses up the educational ladder, the concept of night visitors is educated out of you, and I came to intellectualize and rationalize the true reality of some visitors.

GHOSTLY TRICKS

Some particular entities have never left and continue to manifest from time to time to play little jokes and little tricks on me. Tricks could be objects being moved around or even more dramatic than that.

I had a recent situation where my sister was visiting her son in Washington D.C. She has a condo near where Sherry [Steiger's wife] and I live. One day my sister called from Washington and said that she could see from watching the news broadcast that it was pouring rain back home. She asked me to please check her home.

Now I have a key to her home; she has a key to ours. I keep her key in a special plastic purse in this special box. I told her, I'll check her condo, and I reached for the key. I opened the box, I opened the plastic purse, and the key is gone. What was I going to tell her? What was I going to do? I looked frantically. In my mind, I wondered if I had put it some other place, although that would be highly unlikely. I only kept the key in one place. I found a bunch of keys and mostly hoped one of them would fit her door when I drove all the way over to her condo to test them. I was going out of my mind.

I couldn't check her home. It appeared that I had lost her key. I came home and sat down, wondering how I was going to call her and what I was going to say. There, right on the phone was the key. That's dramatic trickery!

NEVER THINK YOU HAVE ALL THE ANSWERS

I learned the hard way that not all phenomena fit my standard theory of psychic residue. I began writing and publishing when I was fifteen, and my first books came out when I was thirty. The early books were on poltergeists, UFOs, and parapsychology. I wrote a book in 1966 called *ESP, Your Sixth Sense,* and it became a popular textbook in colleges and high schools.

I felt that I had intellectualized such phenomena enough to say what I was most often seeing as a child was really psychic residue that was left in the stagecoach stop, and we probably couldn't interact with the ghosts. So I had a nice theory that I was using to fit every type of haunting. I felt that the ghosts of my childhood had never hurt or harmed me; therefore, I thought ghosts cannot harm people—just frighten them on occasion.

People would call me into their homes because they experienced hauntings. I explained to people that you couldn't interact with these ghosts any more than you could interact with the characters on a television screen or a motion-picture screen. Everything fit within my psychic residue theory. Then, in one particular home I visited, a series of violent murders had taken place over the years, all imitative of one another.

An angry husband had blown his wife to pieces with a twelve-gauge shotgun. This, unfortunately, was repeated by a couple of others spouses who lived in the home ten years later and so forth. This was a house that definitely didn't like people. Something in there hated people.

Yet I was still holding fast to my psychic residue theory. Perhaps the people in the house were absorbing the residue, and they were dramatizing the effects. In that particular case, with my youthful arrogance, at just over thirty years old, I thought I knew everything.

I was in the murder room, and the door kept trying to close. This was an old home where they had once poured cement over a dirt floor, and the door, in order to close, would have to scrape and rub over several uneven ridges in the cement. Yet the door pushed itself over the ridges and tried to lock me into the room. Finally, when I had finished recording and getting any ghostly impressions in there, I walked out and said to my fellow researchers, "All right, close the door. If the blankety-blank thing wants it closed, close it."

We no sooner got upstairs from the murder room in the basement when there was a violent explosion. The door was torn off the hinges. We heard thudding feet coming up the stairs, and then every one of us was lifted into the air and dropped.

I had an epiphany at that moment.

I realized I did not know everything. In this instance, I had dealt with an intelligence that responded angrily to my arrogance and was going to give me my comeuppance. As an individual I don't like categories, but I realize most people do.

Even though I look at the haunting phenomena as a generic force, I do see now that there are different gradations of this force. Some we call crisis apparitions, in which someone we know well appears to us at the moment of his or her death. There are apparitions that are generally of holy figures—the Virgin Mary, Jesus, Buddha—that kind of apparition.

Then there are phantoms, like a phantom woman who walks the side of the road at night. I think across the country we have what we call phantoms because of so many people witnessing and believing in that entity; it simply takes on a life of its own and keeps perpetuating. The more people who see it and get frightened by it, the more energy it has, and the more energy it grows.

I do offer such categories for ghosts and apparitions in my books, like *Shadow World, Beyond Shadow World,* and *Real Ghosts, Restless Spirits, and Haunted Place.* I offer categories so people have a basis of comparison, can identify and recognize the substance of their experiences, and can confirm, "I'm not crazy. I did have a genuine experience that other people have had."

The worldview has come a long way from the time I started speaking on these topics on radio and television. Back then, people lashed out with hostility and anger at me, determined to prove me the fool. Now we turn on the television to see psychic children, mediums, ghost hunters, and more. Now many people have experiences with what I'm referring to as multidimensional entities, from demons or spiritual parasites to angels and spirit guides. Our awareness of other dimensions has opened in the preceding decades.

BUT WHY ARE WE HERE?

My fascination now, as I expressed in my book *Worlds Before Our Own,* is who we are as a species and what is our destiny. Why are we here? I think I have been fortunate to receive some answers why I'm here. When Sherry and I used to lecture a great deal, one of our most popular seminars was on finding your mission. A lot of people asked questions: Why did I come here? Why have I been born? What am I to do?

I challenge readers to go beyond themselves as a species and ask those same questions now that we face a global catastrophe. I'm asking the questions: What is our species? Who is our species? Why is our species here? What are we to learn? What is our destiny and what is our final destination?

The answers are within the mystical experiences for each person, which we must learn to respect and not ridicule. And when our children undergo such experiences, I think parental guidance or mentoring must be there.

I am just going to come out and say it: we must move children away from taking their spiritual blessings as being so special and unique unto them as individuals. Rather, we must teach them to see such spiritual blessings as part of the cosmic inheritance of a great universal brotherhood and sisterhood of which they are valuable members and whose psychic abilities we all share. Children with developing psychic abilities are not mad, insane, special, or new messiahs. Rather, they may represent the future human into which we, as a species, were meant to evolve.

As a species, we are awakening and finally asking questions about who is this species and what will be our destiny.

I've always been a cockeyed optimist. I may still be a little cockeyed, but I'm a little less optimistic. I see we're coming to a time of great choice. We are coming to a time of great decision as a species, and I see that we can elect or choose to become as extinct as the dodo bird. Or we can choose to make that leap in evolution, which when I began writing years ago, was one of the principal hypotheses: we stand on the brink of a great leap forward in our consciousness.

Brad Steiger is not alone in his belief that we live in a time of stimulating ideas and new transformations. Change does cause us to make different choices, and to stretch our beliefs to accept realities like ghosts, even acknowledging that numbers of children who see ghosts are part of our changing environment!

Shaman Lynn Andrews also believes that we live in a time of great change and choices. From the viewpoint of her sacred teachings, which focus on the balance of the physical world with the spiritual one, she posits that each of us must accept greater responsibility for our personal actions and thoughts.

This is precisely why this book offers parents a journey to accept and empower children who see ghosts, no matter how weird they may seem. We can be bolder parents in this time of transformation, seeking information and educating ourselves about moving our children from fear to empowerment.

Lynn Andrews Offers a View of Changes

We are all part of the Great Spirit.
We are all reflections of the Great Spirit.

—LYNN ANDREWS

Lynn Andrews is an internationally acclaimed author and considered a preeminent teacher in the field of personal development. Andrews is a twenty-first-century shaman whose words reflect her heart. I asked about her views on these changing times, what she believes about ghosts and how parents can empower children.

WHY NOW?

If you could, imagine for a moment that the Great Dreamer is awakening. The Great Dreamer or the Creator God that holds up this world and this reality awakens!

This means that you've got to hold up your own reality. That means that the veils of consciousness are thinning, and you're taking over that veil of consciousness. You're taking over your own dreams. So from childhood, at this point, you have to be much more aware today than we've ever had to be. You see?

Now you may be thinking of a very young child that is seeing spirits. So what does that mean? How do you talk to a very young child about taking responsibility for what he or she sees?

I think instead of trying to keep that child from seeing things or trying to explain it away, that child should go deeply into it. I would take a child deeply into it and talk about colors, how they feel when they see a ghost—how they feel it in their body. Do they see colors around the ghost? Does it make them happy, afraid, sad, or all of those things?

I would go into the experience so that a child begins to take responsibility for what he or she sees. I think that's the key issue. We have to become very responsible for the dream, this reality that we carry, and, through acceptance, I think it's possible to work with children at a very young age.

I believe in empowering children: Speak with them. Find out what's going on internally and what that represents for them. Tell stories with each other.

PARALLEL OR ALTERNATE REALITIES

The work that I do as a shaman has to do with a universal consciousness and teaching that has been held here for centuries. The work has to do with the balance of nature—the balance of the physical world with the spiritual world. It has been my experience—and I can only talk about what I have experienced myself—that there are different levels of consciousness.

There are parallel realities, so to speak. My experience has been that you will slip into or through what I call a time warp, a pause in time, and a shift in time, because of your consciousness. [I call this phase shifting or the brain-wave states shifting.] Because of the way that you are thinking at that exact moment, you slip into a level of consciousness that is perhaps a little lighter, less dense than the one in which we live.

A parallel or alternate reality exists right along with the one that we're in right now. The parallel reality exists with a different vibration, to use an overused word, a different *frequency*. We don't perceive it normally because we're not always aware of those frequencies, and we don't phase into them enough. When we go to sleep, we see them. We go to sleep, and we dream every night of our lives. It's part of another world that we perceive when we are in the state of sleep—very low frequency, very slow.

The faster you go spiritually, the slower you go physically. The faster you go physically, the slower you go spiritually. So if you are at a slow, low frequency like a beta or an alpha frequency, you see more spiritually. I say "spiritually," but other levels of reality simply exist right along with us, but in different frequency. So they're not visible.

For a child, who has not had twenty or thirty years of cultural conditioning, those cloaks of experience have not covered him yet. As a young growing person, his mind is open, a lot more open than ours, which become restricted over the years of living in a certain society. Oftentimes, a child will move into a state of consciousness of joy, for instance, and all of a sudden, he sees a shadow going across the room. Suddenly, he sees an angel standing at the foot of the bed, or he might see an animal that he had loved and that died, but then comes back in spirit. I think that happens a lot.

GHOSTS ARE A FACT

I would define a ghost as a figure of energy in a form that we do not normally see or are not used to. Nevertheless this energy form exists and is perceived only when the person seeing it has evolved into some very beautiful areas of consciousness—areas of lesser density than they normally live at.

Ghosts or spirits are a fact. I can't imagine that people don't realize that souls, spirits, whatever you want to call beings from the other side, exist. Children are more perceptive at seeing the other side because they are not as conditioned. If they've come out of abuse, then to get out of a painful situation, a child will go into their imagination, into another plane of existence to escape, and then there will be spirits that they see. I think probably 90 percent of all of us have come out of some sort of emotional or physical abuse. I've worked with people all over the world and have found that to be true. Yet, in a normal household, a child will be happy and joyous and move into a higher realm of consciousness and suddenly see spirits of one kind or another. I think it is a normal and natural process for them to see angels and guardian spirits of all kinds.

Parents may become afraid of these experiences because they think, "Oh my kid is weird. My child is going to grow up with people not liking him. Besides, it can't be true because I can't see it." At that point, a parent should remember that we couldn't see so much of life either when we were children.

ANDREWS'S EXPERIENCE

In my own world, I've always been aware of spirit life all around me. It has been also possible for me to see colors, and I've always seen lights around people. These lights reflect what is happening with the inner body and with the outer body, and seeing them helps me to heal people. I heal with the mind and the heart because I think that a person who is ill has to believe that they are ill. On the other hand, you can also believe that you are healed. If you can make yourself ill, you can make yourself well.

With that same aspect of consciousness, we see ghosts and other parts of reality that may be moving through your field. I always tell people, "Don't get caught in the dream," because in a sense, this earth life is a dream, Collectively we have manufactured this dream as a schoolhouse, a way to learn. This magnificent Mother Earth has given us all the lessons that we'll ever need to understand the cosmos. In a sense, the cosmos, the universe, is within ourselves; it's not outside of ourselves.

I don't expect anybody to believe anything they haven't experienced, but I've seen in my own work that everything is really inside of us. We're always looking outside of ourselves for truth. We look to the Middle East, to the Far East, to Japan, to some guru sitting somewhere in Tibet or in India. We never stop and realize that it's all inside of us. We are already enlightened beings from the time we're born.

So all these different theories are very interesting to me, because I don't know how true they really are. It doesn't matter because anybody can believe whatever he or she wants. I don't want to change somebody's beliefs.

MANAGING REFLECTIONS

Everything that we view in our world is a part of our inner selves from which we learn. The earth is a schoolhouse, and we come here to learn and strengthen our being—what I call the spirit shield—so that when you go to your next lifetime you have become stronger. You are evolving towards the process of heightened awareness.

So the more that children embrace this idea, the more that parents can embrace it and help their children. They're growing in spiritual strength together, no matter what their culture or religion.

With each new experience, you need to impart to your child that they can learn something, and that there is a gift the being or spirit wants to give. Can your child ask the spirit what is offered? Is the spirit walker offering wisdom, or in need of wisdom?

On the other hand, I do feel that we are all made of energy—energy in physical forms or energy in spirit forms.

I think the first lesson of power is that we're all alone.

The last lesson of power is that we're all one.

So in a sense, there is no separation.

Now, I have seen this a couple of times: a spirit could be an aspect of you. If a child is very lonely, they will make up other kids to play with, and they will think those kids are ghosts. That's a different energetic all together. I don't think there's anything wrong with it. If a child is lonely and has a good imagination, he makes up somebody to play with. As a parent, I would observe it and not let it get in the way of children's "normal," regular lives, but there is a gift to every experience.

Psychic Children Become Psychic Adults

One new perception, one fresh thought, one act of surrender, one change of heart, one leap of faith, can change your life forever.

—ROBERT HOLDEN

What Is Normal?

I agree with Brad Steiger's assertion that each of us has our own unique life experiences and coping styles. Seeing ghosts has been defined as paranormal, and for people like Seebo, Steiger, Andrews, and Doreen Fisher and her children, interactions with ghosts are quite normal.

For some stressed children, seeing a spirit may be a healthy way to deal with loss, divorce, or trauma. For Steiger, living in a haunted house and having nightly visitors created associations that he will always remember. For Andrews, seeing colors around people opened her interest in healing

---

4 John Holland, *Psychic Navigator: Harnessing Your Inner Guidance* (Carlsbad, CA: Hay House Publishing, 2003).

energies. For sensitive people who learn intuitively, finding an angel or a guardian seems quite normal and provides comfort to both child and adult. Adults have the same ghost experiences that children have—the ways in which they see may change, but the phenomenon continues.

My Experience

I thought my childhood ghost encounters were onetime events due to stressful circumstances. Only when I grew up did I realize I had a lifetime of such events.

My grandfather Les died when I was eleven. I saw angels around him when I visited him the summer before he passed over. Later that year, two more elderly relatives, a married couple, died within days of each other. When my mother and I visited them in the hospital, I saw angels around them both. I associated angels with death, and seeing them was a beautiful experience, not a horrifying or fearful one. Then I grew up and didn't think about angels, but my ability to see them remained.

Thirty years later, I drove with my parents to visit their very sick friend in the hospital. Toward the end of the visit, I noticed a tall angel standing next to the sick friend's bed. I wished the friend well and followed my parents down the hall toward the exit door. But something held me back—I felt the angel call to me. I was instructed to tell this elder that his time had come. I resisted. I had not shared this part of my adult life with my parents, but neither could I ignore a request from an angel.

I turned back and reentered the friend's hospital room. I took his hand in mine, and with as much love as I could muster, I told him that the angel at his bedside wanted him to know that he would pass over in the morning. The angel knew that the dying man wanted his family to be beside him when he passed, and advised that he call his wife and daughters so they could make the two-hour drive to be with him that night. We both had tears in our eyes as he picked up the phone. His family joined him at his bedside, and his wife later thanked me for heeding the angel's call.

In my interviews with professionals (with the one exception of the skeptic) for this book, I found that those interested in the topic of ghosts usually had personal childhood experiences with spirits—some as vivid as my apparition of the Spanish friar. Almost always, these psychic children did not lose their skills as adults and now use them in service to others like I do.

In this section, you'll read stories from such people as Andye Murphy, Gavin Harrill, Hillary Raimo, John Holland, Sonia Choquette, and P. M. H. Atwater. Their accounts will help parents understand what their children are going through. They also illustrate how childhood encounters with spirits may continue or change through adulthood. You'll learn how different psychics regard spirits and ghosts based upon their experiences. You'll also see how choosing just one definition of the word *ghost* can be confusing. In addition, some storytellers offer tools for empowering yourself and your children when interacting with spirit walkers.

John Holland's Mediumship

It's our adult response to tell kids that it's all in their minds—it's all in their imagination. Children then go on to believe they were wrong, and this is where the seeds of doubt start to grow regarding intuition.[4]

—HILLARY RAIMO

John Holland *(www.JohnHolland.com)* is an internationally renowned medium and spiritual teacher. He has been lecturing, teaching, demonstrating, and reading for private clients for over seventeen years. His weekly radio show is *Spirit Connections*. His story was originally profiled on CBS's *Unsolved Mysteries*.

Holland, who comes from a family of intuitive people, grew up having personal experiences with spirits. He discusses with refreshing candor what parents and children can expect from loved ones who have passed over.

I define a ghost as a person who has passed over and still lingers here, for whatever reason. They don't know they've passed; they're still attached to their possessions. I've even heard that a passed-over heavy drinker might attach himself to a certain place or a bar or someone else who drinks so he can still get the benefits of human drinking. So to me, a ghost is the energy of a person who chooses to stay here or doesn't know that he's passed away.

I think "ghosts" are rare, and I've been in this work over seventeen years. Some people may have a different opinion on it. I can go only by my own experiences and from those that have shared their own stories with me.

I did a television special once on the [1911] fire at the New York City Triangle Shirtwaist Company that claimed the lives of 146 young immigrant workers—one of the worst disasters since the beginning of the Industrial Revolution. There were a lot of tragic deaths there during the fire.

I believe if a traumatic event like that fire happened in a certain area, it leaves a snapshot in the ethers or in the atmosphere. So it's not really a haunting or a ghost. Sensitive people pick up the energy or the vibration of the traumatic event.

The same is true for the soldiers on the Gettysburg battlefield. Are the soldiers really haunting there? I believe that they're caught in a time loop that plays the battlefield scenes over and over again. I think the battle was such a tragic event that it leaves a psychic snapshot.

So encountering a real ghost is pretty rare for me. I deal with people that have already gone. There are other mediums, like the person that the television show *The Ghost Whisperer* is based on, who see ghosts, the trapped ones, all the time. When I say "trapped ones," I mean those that do not know they have passed on, those who refuse to leave, or for some reason, are still attracted to this physical realm.

In my book *Born Knowing*, I answer the question about where the spirit world is because many people ask this. My response is, the spirit world is all around us, but it vibrates at such a high frequency that we can't see it. Earth is the low-frequency place, and I believe there are different levels in the spirit world. What you do here in this physical life will influence where you go in the next. I think there are levels of the spirit world, and I believe that those who have crossed over are at the next level.

Another question people ask me is what spirits do at that level. Well, I've had spirits explain that they're in school or they're helping children. I've had a grandmother sitting on a porch, just looking at her garden. So I believe that the world over there emulates some of what it looks like here, but brighter and clearer, and the colors are more vibrant. Learning seems to continue.

A lot of people think that when you go to the other side, you turn into this exalted being. You don't. You have the same personality.

So the spirit person is in front of me, whether it's in front of a hundred people, a thousand, or one-on-one. I will bring through their personality, whether they were shy, bashful, loud, and arrogant. Do they have that personality still? Maybe not, but they will give me the personality that their loved ones will recognize.

Spirits do not turn into sudden angels when they cross over. A lot of people think that when someone crosses over, they know everything. For example, people say to me, "Ask my father where the will is," or "Have him help me with my finances." If you're dad was awful with money, he's the wrong person to ask for help. Are you calling him just because he's on the other side? You think that he's turned into an accountant? No.

On the other hand, I've had guys come through to their kids and give advice about the crack in the roof or the wall that needs to come down. I say to the person in front of me, "Was your dad a contractor?" When that person replies in the affirmative, then that makes sense. Dad is still concerned and cares. He still knows about contracting, even though he's over there. Mediumship is a fascinating field.

PSYCHIC CHILDREN

I always advise parents in the audience to listen to their children, especially those under seven, who tell the parent that they don't like someone or they're seeing an imaginary playmate. Listen to your child. I believe young kids have one foot in this world and one foot over there. If you want to see a soul in action, watch a child. They're living from the right, creative side of the brain— all imagination and creativity.

When they start school at around seven or eight, here come the books and teachers, and children have to start using the left, analytical side of the brain. A lot of kids could lose their intuitive capacity. Now, a great many others are not losing it. My best advice is to listen to your child. If a child reports a man in his room, don't tell that child, "It's your imagination, stop it, go back to sleep, you're dreaming." Instead ask the child, "What does he look like? Is he saying anything? What is he wearing?" Then take out the photographs of your old relatives. Usually most kids will find that the grandfather, the great uncle, the great aunt is the one they're seeing. In my experience, a lot of them are seeing relatives.

One important way to help fearful children feel safe is to have what I call a safe space, which can be a corner or a room. I felt safe when I started doing my artwork. That's what got me through when I used to see the spirit people in my bedroom. Whether they were guides or relatives, I'm not sure. I used to think I was dreaming, and this didn't frighten me. What scared me most was when my parents told me that my stuffed animals come alive at night. That was scarier to me than the spirits. The sheet would fall on my back or something, or if a sheet moved, I would think it was one of my stuffed animals walking on my back. Freaked me out as a kid. Parents have to be real careful what they tell their children.

> *Places aren't haunted; people are!*
>
> —JAMES VAN PRAAGH

If families move into a house where there was a violent crime, the psychic child, like an antenna, will turn on that psychic loop again. If a house is dormant, and there are no living people in it, the psychic child is the switch for that time loop to start playing. Is the place haunted? I'm not sure. I think it's more of psychic imprints activated by a child's energy. Once that psychic antenna enters the house, it's like a radio. Click, it's on.

When people ask me how to get rid of ghosts, I ask, "Are you sure they're ghosts?" Kids have great imaginations, and most parents intuitively should know when their child is freaking out, when something real is happening, or when the kid is fibbing for attention. I always advise parents, please don't let the kids see how psychics and mediums are portrayed on television, because that's just going to feed into their drama. The most important thing is to listen to your children.

THOSE WHO HAVE PASSED

I think those who have passed have free will to come and go as they please. They want us to not be sad anymore. I use a lot of humor in my demonstrations. I say to people, "Look, I know losing someone isn't funny, whether it's a pet or a person, but they want us to be happy." The main message is, "Stop grieving. I'm okay. I'm right here." The spirits will validate that they're present by telling me what their relative did yesterday or last week.

Once, I read for this big Italian guy and said to him, "Your son is telling me you fixed the chandelier last week." He freaked out because he expected a message like "I love you, Dad." The son's message was too specific—"Yeah, you changed the crystals on the chandelier"—and the father broke down. This big, 280-pound Italian guy says to me, "How could you know that?" I said, "Because he's telling me this!"

That's how I know that those on the other side do check in on us. Our loved ones are just a thought away. That's my favorite saying: "Your loved ones are just a thought away, so put that thought out to them. Those on the other side want to talk to you as much as you want to talk to them."

The process is being aware, and some kids are better antennas than most. I tell parents to get my book *Psychic Navigator*, which guides you to focus on the energy senses and teach your small children to turn down their lights, which are their energy centers.

HOLLAND'S OWN CHILDHOOD

In my own childhood, my gifts were always there. I was born with an artistic ability, winning collage contests for my age group as a child. Out of five kids, I was always the different one. My parents called me the sensitive one. I was a colicky baby. I liked quiet songs as a kid. At seven and eight years old, I read metaphysical books on magic and ghosts and spirits. So I was never afraid because there was something always there, and I believe I've done this before in many lifetimes. So I was born into it.

I was never frightened like some of these kids are; but then again, I didn't have all these ghost shows on television portraying fears and hauntings. My grandmother on the Italian side of my family was a dreamer; my aunt Shirley was too. I've got cousins that know when the phone is going to ring. In my family, the gift was there; it just didn't have a label.

When your grandmother gives you a lottery number, and she calls you and says, "Play four, seven, five," and it comes out in two days, we're like, "Wow, oh my God." We never thought of her as psychic. It was just, "Oh, Grandma dreams numbers."

Spirits Were a Part of Sonia Choquette's Family

When you're dealing with the issue of ghosts, it's really an invitation to revisit the entire paradigm of our perceptions—agreed-upon perceptions. We should no longer look at ghosts as out of the ordinary. What's really out of the ordinary is the fact that we've been so literal and linear and in denial of the multidimensional expressions. Once we begin to recognize that, we can have a choice about what dimension we want to interact with or not. We won't be intruded upon.

—SONIA CHOQUETTE

Sonia Choquette is a revolutionary psychic, alchemist, healer, spirited teacher, and the author of eight best-selling books. Like others I interviewed, Choquette grew up in a family with psychic awareness. She focuses her discussion on the home environment and why children need better emotional boundaries. Her playful attitude helps parents understand how to respond to their children by acting "outside the box," using imagination and creativity. You'll enjoy her explicit instructions in how to help children speak with spirits.

START THE RIGHT CONVERSATIONS EARLY

First of all, let's start with my own experiences. Growing up, my family never referred to ghosts as ghosts. We referred to "disembodied souls" as spirits instead of ghosts. I think the connotation of *ghost* is so negative in our culture. The first obstacle is the vernacular, and you need to change the wording. It's just like the word *psychic* is frightening, but *intuition* is not.

I think if parents really want to help their children become comfortable with the nonphysical world and nonphysical expressions in that world, then they need to root out words that they can't fight in social culture. I mean, ghosts are on TV. Ghosts are in movies. Ghosts are in the group collective mind as a scary thing that is too big to fight.

Let's start talking very early with children and tell them that there's a physical world and that the spirit moves in and out of the body. Just like you can talk to me on the phone, but you don't see me on the phone, the spirit world exists, but we don't see it because our minds become so focused on this plane.

Children's minds are still focused on more than this plane. Their perception's haven't been modified as much to the third-dimension earth. So you tell kids, "Well, you still have your spirit eyes. We all started out with them, but sadly we lose them. Lucky you. You still have them."

That's how I was raised, and it's how I raised my children. In fact, in our home we set the table for the resident visiting spirit. We always had one extra setting at the table for the angel, or the passed-over grandmother, or spirit guide who would be helping us at that time. Spirits were never outside the realm of natural, as their existence was so integrated in my life as a matter of course.

So my first line of support is to suggest that we speak of the spirit or nonphysical world with the same degree of ease as we speak of the seen world. With that phrasing, parents can say, "Some people in the spirit world got lost. They forgot to go home to God. They're lost. So sometimes they're around, and if you ever see one, you tell them to go home. Tell them to go back to the light, because that's where a spirit's home is. If you see spirits, they might need your help. You certainly can give them direction."

To explain things in this way helps children feel like they're in control. Then you can continue, "If you see something and it feels uncomfortable, you can send it to the light, and it has to listen to you, because you have the most beautiful power. This is your world and your home and your realm, and they have to listen to you." All of this type of explanation should be integrated into the conversation casually. That should be the casual response to children who do bring it up.

FRIGHTENED PARENTS

Parents who are frightened are parents who are either poorly educated or uneducated about the spirit world. The first point is your children are intuitive. No matter what you say, they're going to pick up on fearful feelings. Help children by becoming more positively informed: Read books about people who have crossed over. Read about the spirit world; recognize it's just like the airwaves.

We're speaking on this frequency. There's probably 100 billion other frequencies going across the airwaves, and if you're

driving across town, your cell phone might accidentally intercept another frequency. All of a sudden someone else's voice is
on your phone for a brief moment.

It's the same with your eyes. They have the ability to operate
on a certain frequency, and every once in a while they phase to a
higher frequency. That's where you intercept the ghost experience,
which is happening all the time, and your eyes popped into it.

You're just intercepting something here that can't hurt you
and can't harm you, but it doesn't have to intrude. Always ask
the ghost to leave if you're uncomfortable; bless the ghost and
send him to the light no matter what. Tell kids, "If you see a
ghost just say, 'Oh, you must be lost. I'm sending you to the
light.'" They're not harmful.

Parents may find it helpful to teach their children that they
have boundaries, that they have rights to boundaries. I think
the reason some teenagers see ghosts and can't get rid of them
is that their fundamental sense of boundaries is so eroded. The
real issue here is misunderstood. It's not that you can't get rid
of a ghost—it's that you've disappeared yourself. The real issue
to work on, if you're an adult, is establishing your own healthy
sense of boundaries.

So with children, the earlier we teach about boundaries and
the energy fields that protect us, the earlier we can help them
make a choice not to be infiltrated. But if parents have poor
boundaries, kids will reflect that. With poor boundaries, you're
not going to feel empowered to dismiss a spirit.

You must realize that your own energy field is expanded. It's
like you've become the glass of water without the glass. You've
expanded your energy field, and then you're wondering why you
can't get rid of the ghost; in fact, the reality is that you need to
learn to come back into your own frequency and be grounded. Be
in your own body, in your own space, and in the present time.

Children who see ghosts are often in an expanded energy with very poor boundaries, and they often have a desire to not be in the present. Perhaps there's a sense of tension or discomfort in the home that they don't quite know how to deal with. It's often psychic tension. So that's more likely what's going on than the ghost actually reassembling in the third dimension.

So the topic of ghosts in a household begs the question, What is the general atmosphere? Are there secrets? Is there anger? Is there emotional toxicity that's not being discussed or acknowledged and that the children are intuitively picking up and feeling the need to escape? Therefore, they're actually leaving their own bodies. (When you get into the fourth dimension, it's not necessarily the highest frequency of ghosts. It's sort of like the Greyhound bus station.)

But I really believe that [children's ghost sightings are] 99.9 percent motivated by the emotional atmosphere—that somehow the atmosphere does not feel energetically safe for the child in the first place.

The other thing is their parents are not being authentic with them. Yes, I find that parents are not authentic with their children. They say everything's fine when it's not. They say there's no problem when there's a problem. And so children are immediately thrown into chaos about what their own senses are revealing to them, and then they have to escape.

The situation is like trying to scan stations on the radio. If there's dissonance in this vibration, you start scanning to find an open radio station that conveys a little bit more grounded frequency. Children often end up at the bus-station dimension with ghosts.

I think that if your child is grounded and safe, has tools and a sense of healthy boundaries, he or she can live in an authentic way. Why? Being human means we're going to have problems, and the family incubator is where they all percolate. However, we can be real and authentic with each other.

You don't have to elaborate. You can say, "Yes, your father and I are in a disagreement, and it's very uncomfortable right now. I'm sorry. And you're right, it's creating a negative energy, so let's at least calm you down, because you're safe and we both love you, child."

To me, most of the ghost experiences are distractions. We're not here to have a lot of ghost experiences. We're here to be present in this realm. If we pick up the spirit guides, especially as children, there's often two sorts: the kind we find when we pop into the bus station to escape from an uncomfortable or toxic household, or the kind we encounter when we're teenagers feeling in a hormonal disarray. Often emotionally, they're feeling very unsafe.

We can create an atmosphere that explains the many frequencies out there. The frequency that is most important for us is right here. We can be helped and supported by other frequencies, but they will not override our free will.

When there's a ghost in our house, what part of us is vulnerable? Where are we not being honest with each other or ourselves? We need to look at what is vulnerable. I have worked with people for a long time, and I find parents don't come to tell ghost stories unless the children are really the messengers to the parents that something is terribly wrong.

We fear the unknown. So educate yourself. And don't be attracted to drama over information. Like I tell my clients, have you ever been in a blackout? You're sitting in your own living room, and all of a sudden the lights go out. You're scared, but you're still sitting on your own couch. Nothing's changed but the perspective. Then when the lights come back on, you're relieved again. So you have to put the light of guidance on what's scaring you, because the basic thing about ghosts that we're afraid of is that they're going to take over, possess us, and make us crazy and ruin our lives.

Why do people believe they have no choice in the matter? You do! No choice is an understandable perception, given the Hollywood depictions like the *Attack of the Zombies*, and this garbage that we've been fed that goes into our subconscious minds when we're eight, nine, ten, eleven, twelve, and we're watching those movies. So we've actually integrated some of that Hollywood hype as reality.

We must begin to recognize our spirit body, our aura, our free will, our energy fields, our sympathetic systems, the power of decision, and we must acknowledge that there's more than the physical plane happening. Just like you wouldn't just throw your doors and windows open on the street and let anybody wander in, psychically, you don't have to give ghosts a right to wander in. But I still have to say that most of kids' ghost encounters are kids wandering into the ghost realm, rather than ghosts wandering into the kid's realm.

I think that humor instead of drama, and the message that there are things going on around us that our eyes tune out or don't see, helps children understand and lighten up. A child has a better radio station for picking up on the nonphysical world than I do as a parent, but it doesn't mean it's not there for me. It just means my hardware, called my physical eyes, can't quite tune in that subtly yet. Or I've lost the capacity to tune in.

DIMENSIONS

If earth is the third dimension, then we also have the fourth dimension and the fifth dimension. I like to call the fourth dimension the Greyhound bus-station dimension. Everything's passing through—higher forms, lower forms, half forms, thought forms, lost souls. And then you have sort of the sky lounge, the fifth dimension, where you've got the high elementals, the teachers, guides, helpers, and their frequency is really rooted in unconditional love. They're in service to the divine harmony and unity of our great Creator.

Just as there are different frequencies on the radio, there are these different frequencies on the spirit plane. Now, because we're sympathetic, we will tap into where we are. Children often tap into the fourth dimension because they're escaping dissonance here, so they'll get dissonant energies there.

If you're in a peaceful meditative state, you might tune into a beautiful angelic presence or a high guide who appears. So they're both right. It's like the Wild West for most of us. The Wild West has mountains and valleys or beautiful regions and certain areas that are just sketchy.

Finally, emphasize for yourself and to your child that the most powerful spirit is the Holy Spirit—the divine life force, the blessed grace of God that is in our hearts. If we strengthen that, anything that is not that will either assimilate and support the light or go away. So it's sort of the insurance policy to not be intruded upon. And in strengthening that light—and strengthening that wisdom, that clarity—the riffraff, if you will, of the psychic planes will not be a problem.

Melissa Peil Shares Two Stories

Intuitive medium Melissa Peil *(www.mysticalawakenings.com)* was an intuitive spiritual child who reconnected with her talent after the passing of her grandfather. She shares these stories as examples of how one mom handles situations with spirits.

A family whose two-and-a-half-year-old son, Aaron, was seeing spirits asked me for help. Kathleen, a concerned mother, said that her son cried out in the middle of the night because "the man" was in his room. She asked where it was, and he pointed right to where she was standing. She told him he was safe and said to tell the man to go away. The man was still there and left only after Kathleen told the man to go away. Her son went right back to sleep.

Aaron continued seeing a man over a few weeks. Sometimes the man would appear in Aaron's room, but most of the sightings would happen in Kathleen's bedroom. One time, Aaron even saw a dog with the man, and the dog was lying in an empty laundry basket!

Naturally, Kathleen was concerned that now this spirit was entering the boy's room at night unwelcomed. Why did he continue to appear in other places? Kathleen wasn't sure whether to believe her son or not, but she did know that the tone Aaron used when describing the man was one of true belief, not make believe, and that Aaron's crying showed he was scared. Aaron was scared, and she wanted to make him feel safe.

The next morning, Kathleen decided to have a conversation with the spirit her son was seeing. She was alone in her bedroom, which is where Aaron had mostly seen the spirit man. She addressed the spirit of the man and told him these guidelines aloud:

• She believed Aaron was indeed seeing him.

• She wanted to support this, but that she didn't want Aaron to be afraid.

- She would remind Aaron that he was safe and encourage him to talk about his visions.

- But she didn't want the man appearing to Aaron at bedtime or in the middle of the night. She preferred that he came during the daytime.

Kathleen sat on the bed in silence for a moment and wondered if there would be some sign that he heard her. Just then, a toy that one of her boys had left in her room lit up out of the blue! It was like the spirit acknowledged that he heard her.

She put Aaron to bed that night, and there was no mention of the man. The man has not bothered Aaron at night, though she does get reports from Aaron periodically that the man and his dog are in the house during the day.

The best thing a parent can do is listen to children. As Kathleen did, she made her child feel safe; she listened (somewhat critically) to her son, but never showed her criticism to him. She embraced what he had to say and took control of the situation by confronting the source of the problem, the spirit of the man, on her own time, away from her children. She set boundaries with the spirit to let him know what was acceptable for their home and what was not. Being open and honest about your expectations with spirits is all one needs to take control of the situation.

After a while, Kathleen really did believe that Aaron was seeing things that she couldn't see because he was asking often to touch things, as if he wanted to figure out if what he was seeing was solid or not.

Aaron had other sightings of spirits in the family's home. He and his mom were coming out of his bedroom after she'd been changing him, and he was looking down the hall toward Kathleen's room. He said, "The daddy holding . . . ," and he kept repeating it like a broken record. They walked into the room, and he just kept repeating it until he was sitting on her bed. Then he said, "The daddy holding little Jack." He was calm. He then said with a big smile on his face that little Jack was coming over to say hi to him. He said little Jack was climbing up on his lap and that the dog was on his lap too. Aaron was so happy! He said the daddy wasn't saying hi to him. Then he said the daddy was holding the baby, and Aaron started to whisper as if he didn't want to wake the baby.

Kathleen asked if the baby was a girl or a boy, and he whispered, "It's a boy." Kathleen asked if he knew the baby's name, and without skipping a beat, he whispered, "His name is Lucas." He was calm through the whole thing and continued, "It's the daddy and mommy and little Jack and the baby." Kathleen said, "And the dog?" He said, "And the dog." That was it.

This conversation astonished Kathleen because that little speech was the most descriptive Aaron had been about the spirits he saw and certainly the longest time he'd been focused on them. Usually Aaron quickly acknowledged the spirit, and then it would be gone.

Other snippets of Aaron's sightings focused around farm animals. He kept talking about a cow in the family's kitchen. He wanted to get a toy out of the back family room, and he wouldn't go through the kitchen to turn on the light because he said the cow was in there. He seemed genuinely frightened, not just playing around. Another time, the family went sledding and later on Aaron said he saw lots of horses in the field. There definitely weren't any horses around, but Kathleen thought the land they were sledding on was an old Native American reservation.

Hillary Raimo Always Understood the Unseen

Hillary Raimo, an intuitive, metaphysical teacher, author, and talk-show host, was pulled between two generations. Her grandfather was a metaphysician, but her parents did not want to discuss such topics. The result was emotional confusion and psychic tension when she tried to share her happy psychic experience facilitated by her grandfather. Raimo's story provides insight into children's emotional struggles.

IS THIS NORMAL FOR A FIVE-YEAR-OLD?

In my five-year-old world, to meet your parents from past lives was a perfectly normal event because my grandfather led me through a past-life regression where I met my "other" parents. From that point forward, I have been able to see lights and auras around people, and I have been seeing, sensing, and communicating with ghosts ever since.

The event that directed the rest of my life started when I visited my grandparents' gorgeous home, Bentley Farm, in upstate New York. My grandfather had a metaphysical side to his life that he kept private since he had worked for the United States government. I know that he was transferred to South America to work with projects like the Peace Corps. Returning to the States meant that his private life remained so until he retired. My grandfather was into meditation. He got involved with the Edgar Cayce Foundation. Most likely he had healing abilities, and he created his own meditations and developed hypnosis CDs for weight loss and health.

He held our hypnosis session in his living room at the farm. He induced hypnosis by hooking my finger to a machine that clicked according to my heart rhythm. He showed me how it worked and said, "You know, when you go deeper into meditation, you can slow your heart rate down, and you'll hear the clicking going less and less and less." I was so fascinated by the machine that I sat down on the couch and wanted to try his meditation.

So we went through the process of lowering my heart rate, and I heard the clicking. Next, his guided meditation took me up through the ceiling of the farmhouse, and I looked down. I saw the land as he's naming different sights and landmarks. I could see all of it very clearly. My initial experience of the event was the freedom I felt as we went into the clouds.

Grandfather led me through a meditation technique of walking through a door where I met someone from a past life. When I walked through this door, I saw two people, a woman and a man. They were older and dressed in farm clothes. Behind them were rolling green pastures of farm country.

I was struck by my emotional recognition and feelings for the parents. I knew instantly who they were, although I couldn't recall their names. Absolute love poured from them to me, and I didn't want to leave them. Then Grandfather was guiding me back through the door to his living room, and I was emotional—very sad that I had to leave them. Suddenly my parents' little girl was crying, saying she wanted to go back and obsessively drawing pictures of two other people.

My mom was angry with my grandfather for doing that because she didn't trust the psychic realm or subject in general. She didn't understand the experience my grandfather facilitated and was angry that she wasn't there to observe it. I guess there was a lot of family drama that I am still learning about from my parents. The more I speak about it publicly, the more my parents share different parts of the story.

What I remember is the tremendous love that flooded me from head to toe, but apparently it wasn't such a positive thing for my family. Since I could see colors, auras, lights, and spirits in the nonphysical world, I have learned to work with these over the course of my life—at times, struggling with it.

I had a near-death experience two years ago, and since then, I have accepted the gifts. What none of us knew when I was five was that I would be speaking with my grandfather as one of my spirit guides at a later time in my life.

Now I work with spirits in helping to get their messages to our side as part of my service. My ten-year-old son is sensitive to spirits as well. I feel spirits mostly at night before I go to sleep. I have to sleep with an eye mask, or they are too distracting, as they like to stand at my bedside!

I have learned to do what are called "grid clearings" to keep spirits from coming in hoards. Spirits seem to come in massive numbers once there is an open channel. Some of my experiences with ghosts have been positive, and others have been negative.

WORKING WITH CHILDREN

In today's world, I see parents whose children understand and are part of the paranormal world, or the alternate reality. These are the times my grandfather prepared me for. He guided me only so far in the spirit world, but because of my parents' fears with the whole experience, he wasn't allowed to work in any other ways. Looking back on it now, if I had gone through my experiences with more open-minded parents who had a good relationship with the spirit world, my path may have been easier. Yet we choose our experiences and learn from all of it, don't we?

I grew up feeling very different from other kids, and children today feel just as different because of their spirit connections. I think we carry memories or faint residual energy from other lives when we are born into this one. Our memories may fade or go to sleep over time, but we don't ever lose that connection.

So how do parents today help their children keep their connection open to the spirit world and learn to trust it by listening and believing what they say? I had very intense dreams as a child, and I was told they meant nothing. I recall how that explanation never felt right to me because I knew deep inside me that my dreams were important, at least to me. Children today feel the same.

After awhile, I felt a part of me shut down. So listening and validating what your child says are keys to developing a trust between you and your child. Also, children develop trust in themselves and their intuition. If you doubt what kids feel, so will they.

What happened to me at five opened me to new vistas. I was drawing pictures of pyramids in my diaries at five, six, and seven years old. I knew that I had to go to Egypt and knew that Egypt was to be part of my experience in this lifetime.

Because there was animosity between my parents and my grandfather, I felt the tension, rather than ease, around the topic of my spirit-world connection. If I had had more of my grandfather's guidance to help me through the spirit world, it probably would have been a skill that was highly developed intentionally, right from the start.

What parents can do today with their children who see ghosts is ask questions and figure out together what messages their children might be getting. Your children will feel safer if they know they have a trusted loved one on their side. They are experiencing things that others may not, and it can be a lonely and scary place. So even if you do not see or feel what your child does, sit them down and have a conversation with them about it. And be sure to validate their feelings. With their dreams and intuition, as well as seeing ghosts or communicating with the spirit world, children need a support system that makes them feel more sure about their experiences.

CREATING SACRED SPACE

I feel that we must create a sacred space before we take any action or do healing with children. Within a shared space we can establish trust and center ourselves to deal with fear or any other issue. Parents and children learn to shift and adapt to what comes at them, whether that is spirits or information. So being grounded and centered is the best way for everyone to feel safe physically, emotionally, spiritually, and mentally. Creating sacred space can be as simple as lighting a candle, meditating, and taking several deep breaths to clear the energies of body, mind, and soul.

WORKING TOGETHER

When psychic children are open, you can move them through fear by keeping an open mind and seeking to understand. Children may be especially bright lights, so they are going to draw certain experiences to them. We create a problem because the kids aren't supported in the way that enables them to communicate what's happening, and sometimes it's not clear what they're trying to communicate.

All children need someone in their lives who loves them unconditionally. My grandfather was that figure for me, and as I got older, he always accepted me for who I was, even when I did something really bad in my parents' eyes. His love for me stayed with me my whole life, even in times of hardship. Having unconditional love and support was my backbone in times of need.

SEEING GHOSTS

I see ghosts, especially at night. When I'm about to fall asleep, I'll open my eyes slightly, and I'll see ghosts standing at the end of my bed.

Why are they there? They want to communicate. I've had several experiences when ghosts come through, and I am not in a good place myself. I do not want to communicate with them. If spirits find a clear channel, they try to get through clearly, and if that channel gets too static filled, they move on to find another, or they come back later when the reception is better.

I don't have to act on it all the time, so sometimes I ignore them, and usually they go away. When I do readings for people, spirits come into my space as well. They are very respectful of the person they are able to communicate through. Once in a while there is one that can be difficult, but that's the personality of the ghost and doesn't happen too often.

CLEARING

Several times, like three nights in a row, I was going to sleep without an eye mask and would open my eyes just before I fell asleep. That is my clue someone wants my attention.

Once, at the end of the bed was this dark, short child about ten years old. She stood at the end of my bed, clearly defined as a black silhouette; I couldn't see specific features. Then I fell asleep. This same sequence of events happened three nights in a row. Finally, on the third night, I was like, "I'm open to what you have to say to me, but you need to go if you're not going to communicate something to me." So it left.

But I was downstairs watching TV the next night, and my son, Anthony, came to the top of the stairs and said, "Mom, there's somebody in my room."

"What do you mean?"

And he goes, "There's somebody in my room."

I asked how tall the person was, and he raised his hand to his own ten-year-old height. I said, "Okay, go back to sleep. I'll take care of it." I did a clearing the next day.

The clearing is a smudge of the house. I light incense; I like to use sage. I move around the house in a clockwise fashion, starting with the front door and always traveling to the left until I have covered the whole house. I open up windows on a nice day and let in fresh air.

Another technique is called a grid clearing. I was having a rather interesting adventure with another ghost, and I asked a friend of mine for advice on this particular one. She suggested a ritual that clears the energy grid around you, your home, your property, and a mile outside of your property. So you establish an energy boundary with clear intention to keep ghosts out.

Neither my son nor I saw that silhouette again after making a firm statement, "If you're not of the light, you're not welcome." That statement exemplifies that some ghosts' intentions aren't always of the light. That's where it gets a little tricky. You have to discern whether the intentions of a spirit are good or not.

If the intentions of the ghost are not positive, then the child may be afraid for good reason. As the adult in the situation, the parent takes on the role of investigator to ask some questions. The children can draw their conclusions, as I did at age five. If neither the parent nor child understands, they need to find somebody who does and make sure they feel comfortable around that person.

When people have an encounter with a ghost for the first time, they may question their sanity and ask, "Are these things really happening? Am I imagining it? Can I handle telling my best friend when they tell me I should be committed?" You have to get yourself grounded and centered before you attempt to deal with these spirits

WHAT TO BELIEVE?

I think the most important thing is for parents to know that this is real. That's the hardest point when you're working with kids. For example, I once had a client, a seven-year-old girl in second grade. Her mom insisted something was wrong with her, and she was ready to put her daughter on medication. The child was a daydreamer with a beautiful imagination. Her attention bounced from one place to another. Yet I felt intuitively the girl was fine.

This is about evolution of consciousness: understanding your own level of consciousness and how it's evolving. Your children's consciousness is not yours, but you're responsible for helping shape it. So guess what? Our children are really our greatest teachers in helping us to open our minds and grow.

The Childhoods of Psychic Mentors Andye Murphy and Gavin Harrill

In the Rocky Mountains, two bright lights, Andye Murphy and Gavin Harrill, serve as resources to psychic children and their families. Both grew up having psychic experiences and intuitive gifts, and they are now parents to a sensitive child. They recognized that a unique parenting approach was needed in order to raise their daughter in a manner that kept her connected to her spirit guides. Thus, they formed the Psychic Kids and Teens Support Group (PeeKS Group; *www.PeeKSgroup.com*). One goal of the group is to assist other parents who've realized traditional parenting styles are not working with intuitive children and teens. Another goal is to teach and support these amazing kids discovering and managing the phenomena (for example, seeing spirits) that occur in their lives. Their stories illustrate the early and varied interests that children who see ghosts may have.

GAVIN HARRILL

Gavin Harrill grew up in the 1970s, and his mother influenced his beliefs in guardian angels, spirit guides, and parapsychology. He first experienced the feelings of the psychic world when he and his mother went to metaphysical fairs in Chicago. Harrill was fascinated with energetic healing and spiritual principles. Although raised as a Roman Catholic, he was instantly attracted to the theories, techniques, philosophies, and lifestyles of Eastern cultures. He shares:

> For as long as I remember, I loved reading the wise proverbs of the Buddha, Confucius, and Lao Tzu. When I was ten years old, I came across a copy of *Psychology Today* magazine in the dentist's office, and I was immediately hooked on a cool magazine that covered the whole field of psychology that helped people. I clearly see how my thirst for esoteric knowledge and philosophies led me directly to the field of psychology and parapsychology. Professionally, I became a marriage and family counselor. Personally, I enjoy helping families with children who see spirits.

Harrill is an empathic, intuitive healer, a feeler or clairsentient, who uses the medium of emotions and physiological changes within his body to heal and to communicate with his guides. He "feels" everything around him. He senses the emotions of the people in his physical proximity.

When he was younger and hadn't yet learned how to manage and control his abilities, his angels used to joke with him, calling him a "live wire," because that's exactly how he felt. He'd walk into a cafeteria, grocery store, library, or concert hall (anywhere with lots of people) and be overwhelmed by the energies swirling all around. Without proper protection from people's erratic emotional states, he could become sad, anxious, manic, or even fearful without knowing why the sudden surge of emotions had overcome him.

Be aware if your empathic child feels erratic. Because empathy is Harrill's talent, spirit guides communicate with him through his feelings. He gets "zapped," or feels a tingling sensation in specific parts of his body. He explains,

> Getting zapped on the back of my head means I need to be cautious or be alert; something just happened (or is about to happen) and I need to pay attention. Getting zapped on my left calf muscle, for example, means animals or fairies are present, and they have a message for me. Likewise, getting zapped on my left shoulder means a deceased friend is hanging around, and he wants me to know he's watching over me. This is a constant reminder to me that I'm never alone.

> You may experience the zap sensations where you jump out of your skin from getting chills or feel like a freezing wind gust passes right through you. My angels zap me precisely like that for many reasons, but mostly when I'm being pessimistic or judgmental or going unconscious. They jolt my whole body. I'm often startled and reply, "Well hello, angels. Thank you for getting me out of my head and to quit obsessing and shut off busy thoughts."

A Prayer for Protection

I was recently babysitting for some friends of ours in Boulder, and their little girl wanted to go downstairs. As soon as I opened their basement door, I was overwhelmed by emotions that made me queasy and nauseous. I glanced down the dark stairwell, feeling a presence in the basement, and I decided not to go any further. I left that ghost alone for another day. However, knowing there was a ghost in the basement, I said a protection chant so I would no longer feel its nauseating presence.

I've nurtured relationships with spirit guides, especially with the four well-known archangels: Michael, Gabriel, Raphael, and

Uriel. That day, I called upon Archangel Uriel and surrounded myself and the child with a circle of protection.

ANDYE MURPHY

Andye Murphy works as a shaman and intuitive counselor who sees beyond the veil. Her primary intuitive intelligence is sensing energies and spirits around her. Unlike her husband, Gavin Harrill, who feels spirits, Murphy simply knows spirits are present. This ability is called claircognizance.

However, as a child, she was confused by the strange experiences she had. Not knowing whom to talk with, she remained silent for years, suspended in fear, not wanting to be judged or ridiculed.

Harold the Ghost

Murphy shares this childhood event of one of her early ghost experiences to show that not all ghosts are quiet or need help. You'll see that ghosts like Harold can be disturbing, and most likely felt like the people in "his house" were disturbing his domain. From Andye's story, it would seem that her grandmother tolerated Harold's disturbances. I am not sure I would do the same.

Growing up in Louisiana, rather than staying with babysitters, I spent the summers in Iowa with my grandma, who moved to a new apartment in the heart of town. This apartment was haunted with one particular ghost, whom I called Harold. He would mess with the electronic machines and components, trying to get our attention. He would turn on and off the television and radio.

My grandmother says that Harold freaked her out when she came home one afternoon to see that all of the pots and pans had been taken out of the cabinets and were sitting in a pile in the middle of the kitchen. Harold was a very active ghost. There was nothing quiet about his presence. He obviously wanted us to know he was there.

A Psychic Interest Cultivated Early

If your child shows consistent interest in paranormal stories, books, and television shows, they are likely to seek out ghosts, perhaps in games. Andye's story about her Dad gives us pause to ask ourselves how we express ourselves and discuss spirits with our kids. Does the conversation ever come up?

By age six, I was checking out books on UFOs and ghost stories from the library. Teachers told me I wasn't allowed to read what I was reading and made me shut the books. I could hear them whispering and calling me names behind my back. When I was older, I brought the book *Communion* by Whitley Strieber to school for my book report. This was such a cool book that I wanted to tell others about it. And they all freaked out!

My dad is extremely sensitive, but he won't ever embrace words like *psychic* or *intuitive*. As Dad puts it, he just "gets vibes," but his vibes are always so accurate. As I grew up, my dad was always the role model for me, yet I knew if I ever did have these gifts, I would use them for a higher purpose rather than just bubble-gum entertainment.

In my high school years, we lived in a growing Houston neighborhood. I would go with my family on weekends and check out the model homes in new areas being built. One weekend, we went to a house a few neighborhoods away, and we walked into the master bedroom. Immediately, I was in a cold sweat, absolutely panicked. I couldn't breathe, and my dad had to take me out of the room. As he guided me out of the room he said, "I'm sorry, I should have told you." I found out there had been a triple murder in that very bedroom. My dad was aware of it, and he said, "Yeah, I felt it too, honey."

What Murphy Has Learned about Kids Who See Ghosts

Speaking of families, Murphy relates what she has learned about working with psychic children and their families.

I feel children need aware teachers and mentors. I know that I and other psychic adults I speak with would have loved to have received validation and strategies from a mentor when we were teens—someone telling us these abilities are normal and showing us the way. Many adults who find PeeKS say they wish an organization like PeeKS Group had been around when they were growing up.

Many more children are starting to see and talk to ghosts, which bugs a lot of the parents. Many parents contacting us don't embrace the spiritual side of life and don't believe in things they do not see with their own eyes. So when children want to talk about what they see, the parents dismiss it.

Of course, it's human nature to deny what's happening because it scares people. What's really occurring is a child's experience challenging the parents' belief system. PeeKS Group is a resource that understands the importance of validating what these children and teens are going through. In most cases, the kids aren't making anything up. There are no imaginations great enough to come up with the beautiful and synchronistic stories we hear time and again! I use the following strategies.

If a child sees a spirit, I personalize the experience for them by starting the conversation with the spirit. We learn who the spirit is, why it is here, and what we can do for it.

Spirits come because they need help. They're not coming just to play or to hang out. They need or want something from you. If we start asking questions, we typically can provide help.

Most of the time with families, I'll suggest they talk with the spirit aloud. Parents can validate what's happening by speaking aloud and acknowledging what's going on. Denying it's happening to your child only makes your child withdraw further and feel crazy and isolated.

Wake up, step out of your comfort zone, and do what your child needs to resolve this situation.

A final thought to share: Trust and embrace what your children are saying, and find support for yourself for whatever feels uncomfortable. The seeds of distrust sprout when you tell children that their experiences aren't real. This approach sets self-doubt in motion. There is no bigger disservice we do to our children than to tell them what they are seeing, feeling, hearing, or sensing is not real.

P. M. H. Atwater's Research and Personal Experiences

Can we expect an increase in the interactions with the other side, as Steiger and I have suggested? Will more children and adults see and interact with spirit walkers? What research of people's experiences with the alternate realities can we draw on to discover what is currently happening?

To answer this last question, I asked P. M. H. Atwater to share her research on near-death states. P. M. H. Atwater is an internationally renowned researcher on near-death states; she has served two terms on the board of the International Association of Near Death Studies. Atwater is an author of ten books on her extensive near-death-experience (NDE) research, which has included three thousand children and adults. She is an inspirational speaker and teacher.

There is overlap in the study of children who see ghosts and children and adults who experience near-death states. I invited Atwater to share her views in order to enhance our understanding of the children's near-death experiences and interactions with the other side.

All of our brains are shifting, and I want to start out here with certain facts:

Children see invisible things, or interact with other worlds, or have this intuitive ability. Not only is that normal, but it is also necessary, as you'll see in our discussion.

We're speaking first about the development of the temporal lobes, which happens from the ages of two through six, approximately. This is the birth of imagination. [The brain's temporal lobes are beneath the temples and include areas concerned with speech comprehension.]

The birth of children's imagination involves the temporal lobes taking in and sorting all these different forms, shapes, colors, and sounds, so children can build incredible neural libraries that enable them to have perspective and make comparisons as they grow older. Such experiences give us a solid base for what might be expected of us as we live here on the earth plane.

The development of the temporal lobes is so important. Up to around the age of six, it is primary in the way children see and respond to the world around them. In my research of 277 child experiencers of near-death states—children between the ages of birth to fifteen years—most of my cases clustered within two age spans: one from birth to fifteen months, and the other from three years of age until not quite six. This is significant.

Previous research by a myriad of professionals has long since established that the years of three to five are when most children have invisible friends, are highly psychic, see demons/angels/fairies/aliens, and spend a lot of time in the imaginal worlds.

This is the birth of imagination and absolutely necessary for the growth of a healthy child. What I have been able to establish is that during those same years, in fact—from birth to not quite six—is when the largest number of children appear also to have near-death experiences.

The profound enhancements that can occur with the very young after experiencing the phenomenon raises the question, is it possible to have temporal-lobe expansion *before* temporal-lobe development?

What I'm seeing, as a researcher of near-death states, is that the experiences and talents of the new kids [i.e., millennial children, such as indigo and crystal children] are matching those of near-death kids. These experiences are transformations of consciousness. I think the process is inborn in the new kids. The new kids don't have to change through an experience like a near-death state.

So I'm looking at near-death children as a neutral model to better understand what's happening with our new children. I return repeatedly to the fact that this is *normal* brain development, and if children are going to have a healthy brain, they're going to go through stages like seeing ghosts. We're not talking about imaginings or scary things or fluffy things; we're talking about normal brain development.

I've recommended repeatedly that these kids need mentors. They need to be able to talk to and be listened to by someone they can trust. They need a comfortable person who will say, "Now here are some things to look for to help you recognize what's beneficial and helpful and what's hurtful."

GHOST EXPERIENCES

Atwater credits the spirits that she saw in nature as her saving graces through her troubled childhood. If your child experiences illness or trauma, there is a higher chance that he or she will have contact with a spirit walker. Atwater shares these stories of how other parents have handled their children seeing ghosts.

I know that ghosts have been normal for me all of my life. As a kid, I didn't know what to do with such experiences. I didn't know what they were, I didn't know what they meant, and I was confused by them. But I must say that one of the greatest gifts I was given in this lifetime was a practical, logical mind. Yes, I'm just as psychic as anybody else, but I'm also just as logical and practical as anybody else.

One practical aspect for parents and children today is discernment. I suggest that when seeing a ghost or a spirit, parents always affirm God's protection and positively know that they are safe. Confident, enthusiastic people rarely have any problem with the manifestation of spirit beings. Seventy percent of children's near-death scenarios involve angel visitations. One of the stories I wrote about involves a little boy who, during a near-death experience, saw his father walking into the front door. He ran to his father with arms outstretched, believing that help had been found. His father looked right at him, in the face, then ran right past him, ignoring his pleas. This just crushed this little boy. He grew up feeling that his father did not love him. He didn't realize that he was invisible and his father couldn't see him.

As another story, a woman named Lynn detailed what it was like to be resuscitated and then wake up hours later hooked up to a myriad of tubes. She recalled being unable to speak, but being fascinated by shadows moving among the medical staff. She came to realize that the shadows were people who died there in the hospital. She claimed that it didn't take long before she could watch death take place, to see the soul exit the body, and her doctors became so concerned by this. They released her earlier than normal from the hospital because they felt she was going crazy.

Here is another story about a young boy around six years old. He lived in a two-story house, and every time this boy wanted to go to the bathroom, he had to pass by a closet. Every time he passed this closet, this demon would open the door, rush out, and try to grab him and hurt him. This scared him to death. He complained and complained to his dad and his mom. Some of his family pooh-poohed him.

Finally, his dad told him to do something about it. "Don't let this demon scare you," Dad said, "Do something about it!" So the child decided on a course of action. The next time he went to the bathroom, he picked up a baseball bat, and he took that baseball bat with him. Sure enough, the demon jumped out again. This time the boy raised that bat, and he struck that demon again and again. He said, "You're not gonna hurt me. No one's going to hurt me. I can take care of myself."

He was swinging that bat and that demon disappeared. The boy never had problems with that demon again. For the boy, this was a real lesson in self-confidence, being able to stand up for himself, and believing in the power of his own voice.

HELPING CHILDREN HANDLE PSYCHIC EXPERIENCES

Any child can insist on and demand to experience only that which is for his or her highest good and the highest good of all concerned. And learning how to tell the difference in the voices is very easy to do. Learning those differences puts you on the high road to work with, study from, and expose yourself to only those beings, voices, and energies that are truly for your highest good. You don't have to put up with the other stuff.

To reiterate, this has nothing to do with good or bad; it has everything to do with children being sensitive.

When I'm talking to parents, I say, honor what your child is telling you, because for your child, this is absolutely real. Honor them by listening to what they have to say. Then, through suggestions, help them learn from their experiences. Teach them simple visual meditative techniques that will help them use these kinds of experiences in a positive way.

I sit down with parents who are plagued with ghosts, where the child seems to be out of control, and I talk about possession, because possession is real. Kids can get possessed. If they're on drugs (whether those drugs are legal or illegal doesn't matter), if they are imbibing of alcohol, if they're going through periods of real depression or confusion, they're subject to possession.

That's when we really need to get serious help, so children realize that they are valuable, that we love them or we care for them, and that we can take care of this. That's when good lessons in visualization techniques help children balance their mind, body, and spirit. This is the same visualization that Dr. Norman Shealey is teaching with cancer. He sits down with these kids who have cancer and says, "Okay, now visualize armies attacking the cancerous cells." Sure enough, the cancer begins to leave when children feel they can participate in their healing. You're teaching children how to defend themselves and how to be in charge, and that these voices and these appearances cannot and will not interfere in their lives unless the child lets them do so.

First of all I would say, don't shut anything down. You're not shutting down any temporal lobes. You want to be able to understand and to control your gift so that it works to your advantage instead of your disadvantage.

SPIRIT KEEPERS

Atwater's childhood experiences were troubling, but they gave her reason to forge ahead in life, and even influenced the life choices she made.

I had a lot of interactions, with both demons and angels, with the other worlds when I was growing up.

My family lived on the edge of what we called Rock Creek Canyon, south of Twin Falls, Idaho. It was not a deep canyon, but I thought of it as my canyon. I loved it. We had a high pasture out there where we pastured milk cows, and my job was to bring the milk cows like the Holstein, Blackie, down from the pasture.

On one particular Saturday afternoon, I was there early because I wanted to get out of the house and spend some time alone. I was sitting on a log in the high pasture when these forms started rising from the ground. They built up like a mountain. At the top, their peaks, I envisioned a face and hair. These beings were shaped more like a mountain, but I felt these were people. They were translucent. I could see right through them. They called themselves spirit keepers.

As I became engaged and participated with them, I realized that every point on the earth has a spirit keeper, because the spirit keeper's job is to hold matter together. They are the glue that holds light together intensely enough and firmly enough that we can have matter. Light becomes dense enough that it has that lower vibration and forms matter; the spirit keepers hold that light together so it never falls apart or goes spinning off into the universe. They are that glue or spirit force that enables matter to exist.

As I got acquainted with the spirit keepers, they taught me how to go through a cliff, pass through a rock, and move through other matter. The spirit keepers enabled me to keep my sanity because it was at a time in my life when I was desperately unhappy and had no voice at all. The spirit keepers honored me in a caring way and enabled me to be who I was. They enabled me to make significant turns in my life.

I'm one person, then, who says that the interactions we can have with the invisible worlds are life changing, but can literally give us the information, support, and caring we need to become healthy human beings. That certainly happened in my case with the spirit keepers. I would have never been a healthy human being without them. I would have wound up in prison, because that's where I was headed. I was so enraged and full of hate. I had five fathers and two mothers and wound up raising myself.

The spirit keepers honored my existence. They taught me. They showed me. They enabled me to see who I really was and feel good about that.

You're in charge. You're in charge of your life, so take charge.

"Is My Child Psychic?"

Professionals are often asked, "How do I know if my child is psychic or just having a singular encounter?" Parents of a child who sees or has seen ghosts might be thrilled to discover that their child is psychic, or they might be disturbed by that knowledge. A onetime ghostly event can be triggered by several stressors, like drinking aspartame in diet soda, food allergies, emotional intensity or overload, an emotionally toxic home environment, physical or mental abuse, or night terrors. An adrenal overload of the stress hormone cortisol can activate the temporal lobe, the part of the brain associated with psychic activity. A onetime sighting may also be a crisis apparition, experienced by adults and children alike after the death of someone close to them. If a child has a onetime event, does this mean a child could have other events? Possibly.

Athena Drewes Responds

Athena A. Drewes, Psy.D., RPT-S, is a licensed child psychologist, parapsychologist, and consultant to the Rhine Research Center at Duke University and the Parapsychology Foundation on children's psychic experiences. She has conducted research, written articles and reviews, and spoken on children and ESP. She coauthored, with Sally A. Drucker, the reference work *Parapsychological Research with Children: An Annotated Bibliography* (The Scarecrow Press, 1991). Drewes is also author and editor of five books dealing with play therapy. Her personal experiences shaped her interest in the subject of children who see ghosts or those who exhibit other traits of intuitive intelligence.

Like me, Drewes receives questions from many parents about kids who see ghosts and the correlation, if any, to a child's psychic abilities. These questions include:

Are all children who see ghosts psychic?

Do all psychic children see ghosts?

How can we help these children not be afraid?

How can we help these children feel confident?

DREWES'S PERSONAL PSYCHIC EXPERIENCES

I became interested in the field of parapsychology and psychic phenomena when I was a child. I had many recurring dreams and a sense of past-life information. However, the most out-standing event that crystallized my interest and future career occurred at age ten, when I had a precognitive dream.

I was in bed. I had five pages to go to finish a book, and I really wanted to reach the end before I went to sleep. My mother yelled at me to go to sleep and turn off the light. She then sent in my older brother to shut off the light. I was furious and so angry as I fell asleep. That night I had a lucid dream, in which I was seeing, as an observer from outside of myself, my family being in a car accident. I knew my mother was severely hurt, coming in on a flatbed stretcher with wheels, which I found out later was like a gurney. I saw my older brother, who was my younger of two brothers, but still older than me, sitting in a wheelchair. I knew he was not hurt.

The dream had a special feel, a very profound sense that this was not my usual dream. It stayed with me in vivid detail.

About two weeks later, the family went to see a movie. It was raining, and as we were heading home, a car accident happened. The same exact scenes from my dream replayed before my eyes. It was very striking that I had dreamt this. I told my father at the time, "I just dreamt this accident two weeks ago. The same exact scenes." He turned to me and said, so seriously, "Don't ever tell anyone."

From that age I wondered, how can dreams tell us the future? How can they come true? Moreover, I worried if my anger had caused the accident to occur, which would have been pretty phenomenal by itself. I felt guilt throughout childhood and feared the effects of my anger.

The dream experiences led me toward one part of my professional career: seeking out information about psychic phenomena. There weren't a lot of books or people to turn to. I was hesitant to tell friends about my experiences and had to be selective. They would start to think I was a witch or crazy. Around age nineteen, I read about a study that was being conducted on telepathy-dream research at Maimonides Medical Center in Brooklyn, New York. The research sounded so much like my experience. I had to check it out.

I called the researchers and asked if I could speak with them about their study. They invited me to come down, and I wound up staying the night, running the research experiment with them. I found a whole research group of kindred spirits who knew what I was experiencing. The fact that my dream was a precognitive experience alleviated my sense of guilt.

I had many other psychic experiences growing up, including telepathy. Even in recent years, I have experienced clairvoyance and precognition, and more recently, I'm starting to see spirits and am having a lot of past-life information coming back.

My professional path includes being a researcher with children who have had psychic experiences, writing articles, doing public speaking, and helping children and parents understand their psychic experiences. And I have remained a consultant for the Rhine Research Center in Durham, North Carolina, as well as the Parapsychology Foundation in New York City. The other part of my professional path as a child psychologist is working with children in a variety of settings to help them feel heard and validated about their psychic and emotional experiences.

HELPING PSYCHIC CHILDREN AND THEIR PARENTS

As a consultant, I receive a lot of e-mails from parents and children about their psychic experiences, and I respond to them. I was featured on an A&E show *Psychic Children* back in 2006, and [the A&E show] *Paranormal State* has contacted me to work with a few children. Also the current A&E show *Psychic Children: Children of the Paranormal* has sent me the e-mails from viewers who have concerns about their children or their own personal psychic experiences.

The two worlds are coming together for me now. I'm doing a lot of active consulting and counseling and supporting children to help them understand that their psychic experiences are a gift and not to be afraid of them.

I don't see children making things up. I don't see them fantasizing and creating their experiences for glory or attention. Even imaginary playmates fit in with normal child development, and that's part of children's worlds. But sometimes children are seeing spirits of other children, and they call these spirit children their imaginary playmates. I have never run into a child who I feel is manipulating or utilizing their psychic abilities in any other way than is legitimate.

In the past, the e-mails I received were more around precognitive dreams and a little bit about paranormal, psychic contact with the spirit world, be it seeing actual figures and shapes, hearing other entities, or sensing the essence or energy or orbs of spirit forms. Now the e-mails are almost exclusively in the latter realm. I think people have come to realize parapsychology and psychic phenomena are the norm. Having psychic experiences is not so atypical, but seeing spirits, hearing their children talk about it, and helping children understand how to cope with it are much more relevant topics to parents and of concern for kids at this point in time.

I would say 90 percent of inquiries I receive are from parents who are accepting and open to their child's experiences. I would say maybe 65 or 70 percent of the parents believe in such ability to have contact with the other side, but they are concerned for their child. If they see that their child is in distress, they want help, or they don't want to say or do something to make it worse for them.

BEING PSYCHIC VERSUS BEING PSYCHOTIC

A good 10 to 15 percent of parents are concerned that what their child is experiencing is a psychosis, a psychiatric issue, and they are wondering whether they should pursue medical help. Sometimes, mental-health practitioners or school personnel push parents in that direction. Some parents intuitively feel that's not the thing to do, but they don't want to go the in wrong direction and not seek the help if it is needed.

Let me explain the difference between psychosis and a regular psychic gift. I see the two as qualitatively different. I consider whether a child has had other psychic phenomena occur in their life. What is the quality of what they are saying about the spirit contact? I would encourage the parent to consider a psychiatric or psychological problem and referral to a mental-health professional (e.g., psychologist, social worker) when I hear the parent or the child report that the spirits are telling them to hurt themselves or to hurt others, when the spirits' communication may have a very bizarre feel to it, or when their children's thought processes are not very logical or coherent when they explain their experience.

Stress or other events in the child's life could have triggered these symptoms, and spirit contact may be in there. Yet the children are so overwhelmed and feeling defenseless that they do need some other form of intervention besides just an understanding about the phenomena. They may need medication; they may need psychiatric help.

In a small minority of the requests that I get, there isn't necessarily a spirit contact. With the media shows out there, sometimes the parents are hoping the answers to their questions are going to be more sensational, and they're not.

I have a handout of frequently asked questions, *Is My Child Psychic?*, that lists ways that the parent or child can understand their experiences. They can keep a journal, for example; they can look at psi patterns and write things down. These are ways for the parents to respond matter-of-factly and not give psychic experiences too much emotional power, either in disbelieving or believing, because kids are susceptible to the reactions of their parents.

ATHENA DREWES'S HANDOUT FOR PARENTS

Could My Child Be Psychic?

FREQUENTLY ASKED QUESTIONS

"My four-year-old daughter seems to know what I am thinking. When I was in the kitchen washing dishes and wishing to myself that I had a clean towel to dry them with, she went to the linen closet and brought over a fresh towel without being asked."

"My eight-year-old son is able to tell me who will be calling or dropping by before it happens. So far he hasn't been wrong yet!"

"My teenage daughter has been able to 'talk' with my deceased mother for years and now reports having contact with other spirits who are coming to her."

WHAT IS ESP OR PSI PHENOMENON?

Psi is the ability to perceive and obtain information about the past, present, or future, and about others, events, and situations, beyond information available to the ordinary five physical senses. Often psi has been referred to as the sixth sense or extrasensory perception (ESP). It is also often considered paranormal (something that happens, but seems impossible).

There are several different categories that have been researched over the past seventy years by parapsychologists (scientists who study the paranormal):

Clairvoyance: extrasensory knowledge about objects, places, or events happening at a distance.

Precognition: prediction of random future events through dreams, waking images, thoughts, or knowledge that cannot be inferred from present information.

Psychokinesis (PK): direct mental, but not physical, influence exerted by an individual onto a physical condition or object.

Telepathy: the simultaneous extrasensory knowledge of another's thoughts, mental state, or activity.

Mediumship: the ability to see and/or hear discarnate spirits or make some paranormal events occur while communicating with the dead.

Remote sensing or viewing: using ESP to see or hear something far away.

HOW DID MY CHILD GET TO BE PSYCHIC?

A child or teen who displays paranormal abilities is not odd or weird. The child or teen should be thought of as being talented in a particular area, but he or she looks, acts, and plays like any other child. The difference is that the psychic abilities are often so pronounced that they cannot be hidden. The child cannot deny them and may have unusual sensitivities, such as being more affected by a casual rejection or emotional experience, or being more reactive to the emotionally confusing states of others.

Research has not been able to find a specific reason for or a source of such abilities. It is possible that there is a genetic component, as many families report that other family members have similar abilities. It may be that each of us has such abilities, but some have them more strongly than others, just as is true of other talents, such as drawing or playing a musical instrument.

ARE CHILDREN OR TEENS MORE PSYCHIC THAN ADULTS?

Children appear more open-minded and less skeptical about such experiences, and as a result, children may talk more about them. However, research has not found that any one age group has more psychic ability than another.

ARE THERE BOOKS WHERE I CAN READ
MORE ABOUT ESP AND CHILDREN?

The Gift. ESP, the Extraordinary Experiences of Ordinary People. Sally Rhine Feather and Michael Schmicker (ISBN: 0-312-32919-9)

Is Your Child Psychic? Alex Tanous and Katherine Fair Donnelly (ISBN: 0-59510064-3)

Psychic Children. Samuel H. Young (ISBN: 0-38507958-3)

Raising Intuitive Children. Caron Goode and Tara Paterson (ISBN: 978-1601630513)

HOW SHOULD I RESPOND TO MY CHILD'S PSYCHIC EXPERIENCES?

1. Listen to your child without judgment or ridicule. Create an environment of acceptance, understanding, and caring, so that your child will not be afraid to speak about their experiences. Allow your child to talk freely about their experiences. Casual comments such as "Oh, you picked up what I was thinking," "Isn't that interesting?" or "Tell me more about your dream and why you think it will come true" help the child to open up.

2. Normalize the experience. Let your child know that other children and even adults have similar experiences and research has been conducted on such experiences. Let your child know there are places to get answers to their questions if they want. (See www.parapsychology.org; www.rhine.org; www.aspr.com; www.parapsych.org.)

3. Do not force the child to "perform" their abilities. Children's psi experiences will often be spontaneous, and the child will most likely not be able to control such events at will. Never focus on using psychic abilities for personal gain or show. Such approaches may actually cause abilities to decline, result in children feeling exploited, lead to an inflated sense of ability, or force children into resorting to fraudulent activities to keep the attention on them.

4. Put psychic abilities in perspective. Children should be helped to understand that while they may have psychic abilities, they have

other things to learn and other talents to develop. Let your child be a child, not treated as a little adult. Encourage your children to develop all their abilities and to see that their psychic abilities are like any other talent or skill that people have, like being a gifted pianist, composer, artist, actor, or athlete.

5. Keep communication open. If your child tells you about a psychic experience, accept what has happened, whether you believe in it or not. If a child's statements are received negatively, your child may not approach you again about any other experience, psychic or not. They may try to suppress their abilities, lose creativity, withdraw, or develop feelings of distrust and anger.

6. Keep a journal of psi experiences. Encourage your child to record such events or dreams. Write down what happened as soon as possible after an experience occurs, to keep information fresh and get the most details as possible. Over time patterns may emerge. Journal writing also helps you decide which category the experience belongs in, and whether the information received in the experience was accurate or not. Try to add documentation after precognitive or clairvoyant events occur to see how accurate details were and how long it took before the predicted details "came true." Record the times the events did not seem to occur or significant details were missed. Often psychic impressions come through when there is minimal interference and the conscious mind is not distracted by other things, such as during sleep, during car rides, or during daydreaming. Often the content of events is about friends and everyday things or family members.

7. Try out simple ESP games. Use guessing games to see if your child can draw a picture of an item or say the word that you are

thinking of. Have twenty-five M&M candies, five each of five colors (red, green, blue, yellow, brown) in a brown paper bag; select one candy, hold it inside the bag, and see if your child can guess which color will come out. Then put the candy back in the bag, shake the candies up, and repeat the procedure again for a total of twenty-five times. Record each candy selected and your child's response. A score of five correct out of twenty-five is considered chance—the usual number when no psi phenomena may be occurring. A score of seven or higher or four or below can indicate psychic abilities.

Athena A. Drewes, PsyD
Licensed Child Psychologist
Consulting Psychologist and Parapsychologist
For further information or to contact the author: adrewes@hvc.rr.com

STEPS THAT HELP KIDS

First I let parents and children know that they shouldn't be afraid of the spirits and that spirits are not going to hurt them. Kids can keep a night-light on in their room or turn on the light from a fish tank, which changes the energy pattern in their room, so they will have less contact at bedtime and when they're sleeping. For some, that is very helpful and solves the problem.

For older teens, sometimes lights aren't as effective because they still feel the presence strongly. I give them, and any child who may feel afraid, a guided-imagery meditation in which I have them do some deep breathing. I ask them to close their eyes, put their feet on the ground, and envision that they have a bubble around them. The bubble is filled with white light, and it's the white light of God's love or universal love or the energy of the universe (depending on their religious beliefs). It protects them. Whatever is on the other side of the bubble is not going to harm them. As they breathe in, they breathe in that love and energy and feel it envelop them in that bubble. As they breathe out, they expand the bubble beyond them into their room. And then as they breathe in again, they feel the protection of the energy and love. Then they breathe out and expand the bubble out to fill the whole room, then again to fill their house or apartment, and then to expand the bubble out into the universe. This is done so they don't keep their aura, their bubble so tight around them—so that their aura is really out there.

Once a mother asked me, "Do you ever teach any defensive techniques?" I do tell the children that they can tell the spirits to leave them alone and to go away; they can command spirits to leave. Practice and role-play this scenario together. Children can practice saying, with their very loud voice, "Go away," just like they would say it to anyone who's bothering them in the real world.

Let children know that they have a right to their space, to their protection, to their body, and certainly they can say, "Go away and leave me alone." I also teach them, even in their meditation, to send love to the spirit and to say, "You need to move on, move to the light, move to the love. There's someone waiting to help you cross over. You don't need to be here."

I help children understand that a spirit is not a malevolent, evil thing. A soul or spirit may be lost and may come to children because they are open and sensitive. And the spirit could be that of a child. I tell children, "You can send them on their way. You don't need to have them around you."

Most of the kids do sense their guardian angels, relatives, and people who are there to support them, rather than lost spirits. Yet as kids get to be ten, eleven, or twelve, and during puberty, they tend to develop their abilities more. Other psychic abilities come forward.

Their emotional states are a little unbalanced. So kids in that age range and the teen group are those that I really want to work with. Working on the fear factor is most important because fear attracts the negative, fearful, or intense energy. It is better for tweens and teens to learn to send out love, but also not to invite the negative to them, either through thinking, "I've got all these super powers" or "I'm the greatest here."

If a child is feeling emotionally unsettled, they can move into a direction that is negative and can add to a greater psychological imbalance. So our role is to definitely empower them, to help them role-play and practice sending the spirit away, to not fear it.

In fact, they need to feel less fear and know they are safe. I also tell kids, depending again on their religious beliefs, to call on Archangel Michael. He's the warrior archangel who will protect. Some parents have pictures or icons of Archangel Michael near them. I then tell children, "Call on your spirit guides or angels to protect you and keep you safe. There are people looking out for you."

RESEARCH

You can set up ways of helping children tune in to their psychic abilities. I had conducted some studies with children and using M&Ms as a game. We had five M&Ms each of five different colors—red, green, yellow, orange, brown—so there are a total of twenty-five. You put the M&Ms in a non-see-through brown bag, shake them up, pick one, and hold it inside the bag. The child guesses what color M&M is in your hand, and then you take out the candy and record its color. Then you put the candy back in the bag and repeat. You do this twenty-five times.

Chance says five correct answers would occur. So any score above five, usually seven and above, starts to be beyond chance—more than just the normal guessing. From the parapsychological view, there is some psychic ability that the children are tapping into and using for the information.

The parents could also be behind a screen, looking at the M&M color and having the child guess. We found some significant results in children similar to those Dr. J. B. Rhine got when he started the field of parapsychology using Zener cards, in which there were five cards each of five different symbols. He did a lot of card tests with everyday people and with people who were psychic or mediums or known to have some ability. Children are as psychic as adults are.

I believe personally we're all psychic, and some more so than others. It's just like being able to play the piano. Some, like Mozart, are virtuosos at a young age. Some have to work hard at it and develop their skills, and some could care less about their psychic abilities or information coming to them.

Children have psychic abilities. Some of the testing we did certainly shows that. Children also have some of the same personality characteristics as adults in terms of being open, positive thinkers. If you have a negative view of things, we call that the sheep-and-goat effect. If you are more believing, like a sheep is, you tend to be a higher scorer on psychic ESP tests. If you are a goat, a nonbeliever, you actually tend to score in the negative range.

On a psychic test, if a child is getting twos or threes, this says they're suppressing their psychic ability. Normally they would have gotten five just by chance, so something's occurring to suppress their information.

Some of the research is inconclusive as to whether children lessen their psychic abilities or put a kind of shield over it as they enter school. My personal view, from my own experience, is that when you're under the age of five, you don't really censor what you say. You believe everything. You're open to all possibilities. You're very in tune to the other side, and so you share it all. You tell your parents. You tell people close to you. If they're accepting and open, you continue talking about it.

But when you get into school, the world changes. Then you find out people are not so open to hearing about psychic experiences. Then the teacher calls your parent up and says, "Your child's been talking about seeing spirits. I think you need to go see a therapist or a psychiatrist." Kids start teasing you, making fun of you, expecting you to perform on command, or get frightened by what they hear, because that's not what they believe or what their parents tell them.

The child starts to shut down by not talking about it, or you get a direct verbal statement from a parent, like my father, "Don't ever tell anyone," as though there's something wrong with it, or you should be ashamed of it, or you'll be viewed as a witch. Sometimes the abilities go undercover and get suppressed.

Sometimes children mask or shield their gifts because they're frightened of them. Then when they hit puberty hormonally, you see a rise in psychic ability.

There's a lot of research being done at the University of Virginia in the field of parapsychology, on out-of-body experiences, past lives, and near-death experiences. Dr. Melvin Morse wrote about children having near-death experiences with very similar aspects to those in adult reports.

AN INCREASE IN THE EVOLUTION OF PSYCHIC SKILLS

A lot of the people I encounter through e-mail, lectures, and workshops believe their experiences are real. They have sensed spirits and had personal experiences, or they believe their children and wonder, what does it all mean? Where does it all fit?

I feel that reports of spirit contact and psychic abilities are increasing within children. What the source or causes are, I don't know. I leave it up to others to draw their own conclusions. I have my own personal view that a shift in consciousness is occurring. It depends on your philosophy and whether you believe in reincarnation, which I do. We are here for a purpose, and we are all coming together for a purpose. For me, I see it as my role to help children understand and master what they are experiencing and not to be afraid of it.

I think the most important thing to underscore and emphasize again for children and parents not to be afraid of what the children are experiencing or being told. It's important for parents to really support their child and be a resource for them to come to; to allow their child, even if they don't believe this, to have a place to come and talk and to share their experiences;

to help center their child and ground them and anchor them in their love; to help their child realize that they may be seeing things or feeling things that the parent can't, and that's okay. You want to be there to hear them and help them.

The worst things that a parent can do are to shut the door and to turn their child away and not allow them that forum. Turning their child away has more negative emotional consequences for the child, especially as they grow up. And it shuts the door to other important communications that are not about being psychic. The child feels that you are not a person that they can come to, because you cannot truly hear them. So the most important thing is for the parent to be loving and accepting, and for the child not to fear and not to give in to their fear—to feel the love, that they are protected, and that they are safe.

How Parents' Beliefs Affect Kids Who See Ghosts

All of us bring to our parenting the good and the bad of how we were parented, our coping skills based upon the adversity we have faced, and our expectations of how our children should be. This is great! We can pick the positive parenting strategies that helped us grow wisely. We can discover what inner strength or coping skill got us through the bad times. The more confident we feel as a parent, the safer our children feel with us.

What we bring to the table as positive parents are the strengths that got us here, today, now reading a book about how to help a child who sees ghosts—curiosity, intelligence, desire to learn, desire to help, intuition, and the desire to inspire our beautiful children. On the other hand, we also pass along our fears and shortcomings.

With that in mind, this section first discusses how children develop their personal worldview based upon their interactions with parents. Then we answer the question of whether or not you have to believe in ghosts if your child sees them, and how to better understand your child's fear. Next, Dr. Robert Flower, a world-renowned expert in the science of thinking and achievement, covers three levels of thinking, and notes the one which provides for personal growth and acceptance of new and different ideas. Finally, skeptic Joe Nickell presents a logical approach for exploring the topic of kids who see ghosts. Read all the viewpoints in this book, and you'll have a whole picture.

Michael Mendizza on Brain-Wave States and the Ability to See Ghosts

Your success or failure in anything, large or small, will depend on your programming, what you accept from others and what you say when you talk to yourself. . . . It makes no difference whether you believe it or not. The brain simply believes what you tell it most.

—RICHARD HELMSTETTER

To discuss how children develop their self-worldview, I asked author Michael Mendizza to discuss children's brain-wave states and their relationship to what children see. Mendizza is an educational coauthor of *Magical Parent Magical Child: The Art of Joyful Parenting* and founder of *Touch the Future*, a nonprofit learning-design center.

GHOSTS AND THE ELECTROMAGNETIC SPECTRUM

What is the relationship among brain waves, what children see, and spirit walkers? Why do young children see things that grown-ups don't see? Most adults don't see entities that the general culture does not recognize. Yet if children were raised in cultures that do recognize spirits, then children and adults would both see them.

EARLY NEURAL NETWORKS

I am quite interested in the notion of who we *think* we are. My coauthor, Joe Pearce, defines a factor called the self-worldview, which influences whether or not we see other aspects of the electromagnetic spectrum.

The self-worldview is the embodied state and the culture it gives rise to. By interacting with the environment, a child's brain activates and develops only the potential networks that match or prove to be useful in the environment. Whether or not you see a "ghost" is the function of the inherent potential that the body is genetically sensitive to, plus the filters that are imposed by culture.

In the early years, between ages two to six, the brain has not distilled enough to distinguish between conception/perception that is inner generated and outer generated. It is usually during this time that young children experience and develop relationships with invisible friends and what we might call ghosts.

Between ages seven and eleven, the brain comes to a different order, and the dreamy influence of early childhood diminishes in most children. At age eleven, the brain flushes and dissolves the unused potential neural networks, fixing the brain in its current relationship with the environment. This effectively prevents any perception experience that is not in sync with the child's or family's environment/model/culture. Thus, a lot of children may no longer see ghosts, energy forms, or spirits after puberty.

If the child sees a form or something that the adult doesn't see, they quickly learn to screen that out or hide it, because that's not normal in their parents' environment. The ghost is not part of what the culture reflects; it's not part of the bonded experience. It would be an unbonded experience for the child to see forms that the parent doesn't see.

"Bonding" refers to a shared meaning. I'm using the word "bonded" in the sense of the shared meaning of "ghost" between adult and child. A parent and child are constantly rechecking in with one another to say, "Do you understand? Do you see what I see?" That's part of renewing the bond of sharing a worldview, establishing the social network.

In a situation of unbonding—something not shared—the child sees something like Harvey the Rabbit and the parent doesn't see the rabbit. The child will quickly be suspicious of that rabbit and will stop talking with the rabbit in front of the parent. Then the child's brain is going to "normalize" to what is culturally accepted. That normalization process screens out these vast potentialities that are basically unrecognized by the culture—the unsupported and unrecognized electromagnetic spectrums.

So we have these different brain frequencies as the brain goes through its stages of growth and development; it changes and adds higher frequencies or different frequencies to its brain-wave patterns, which correspond to states of perception.

The interesting thing that my coauthor Joe Pearce is pointing out is that if the adult culture saw what we call ghosts, the kids would grow up seeing ghosts too. If the adult culture doesn't see ghosts, then the child doesn't have what Joe calls a model to mirror.

Then at ages eleven to fourteen, the brain goes through this big cleansing process and physically dissolves the unmyelinated potential neural connections that were available in the early brain. We either use it or lose it, and by age eleven, nature assumes that you are going to be using everything that the environment calls for you to use. It says, "We don't need this extra stuff. Let's clean house and wash it away." There's this big flushing sound that goes on in the brain; again, it distills to a new order. At that point, most people stop "seeing."

What we call "psychic" is absolutely normal for that early brain that has all these networks and is wide open. Then after the wash and the flush, because we have diminished our potential, we look back and say, "Oh, that's psychic, that's extra, that's not normal." But psychic, I'm saying, is quite normal.

THE ADULT STATE IS THE IMPERATIVE MODEL

The state of the adult becomes the cookie cutter or model that the child's brain adapts to. Einstein, for example, didn't talk until he was four or five. He had this great imagination as a kid. Did he spend most of his time in abstract realms of thought? Most kids have great imaginations, and then basically, most kids are beaten out of their imagination. They are told to get real, do it this way, do it that way, don't imagine, and just do it by the numbers.

So the adult culture shuts down their imaginative structure, and then they move into later stages of development, having diminished this core capacity called the imagination. They've let it atrophy and get retarded, and then they move into adulthood with a retarded imagination. Well, Einstein did not shut down that potential. What made him a genius was that he continued to bring that imagination into more adult realms of possibility. By the time he became an adult, we considered him a genius. But had he shut down, like most people have because the adult culture enforces that, he would have lost what Ashley Montague calls the "childlike genius."

The self-worldview becomes the handbook, the guide that determines how we relate to the world—how we see, experience, understand, interpret, and respond to the world. So the self-worldview becomes the *whole map*. The whole human experience is being defined by the self-worldview that we are imprinting.

The point that I am certainly passionate about is that that self-worldview that we call normal is really a retarded one—clamped down, narrow, acculturated. Then you get religious overlays, parental overlays—all of which become part of our identification. Our self-worldview is paltry compared to what our potential is.

Krishnamurti, whom I knew very well, made this wonderful clear statement that because we don't know who we are, we're destroying the planet and ourselves. And frankly, I've never heard anything that is so big and so accurate as that statement. It focuses attention on the inner world, not on the outward world, like financial markets and politics.

Unless we grow up, discover who we really are, and know our right place in the world or universe, rather than who we *think* we are—this acculturated process—we will continue to destroy each other and the planet. We're doing it so well that we don't have much time.

There's nothing that's going to change because everything is being reconstructed out of our same self-worldview. Unless we change our self-worldview, which is the hardest thing in the world to do, we're toast.

"Do I Need to Believe in Ghosts to Help My Child?"

I hope you see the importance of parental influence on a child's self-worldview. When a child sees a ghost, he or she turns to mom or dad for support, problem solving, or a fix to the situation. How a parent responds will influence the child for the rest of his or her life. Yes, that is true for all life events, but how a parent handles kids seeing ghosts is especially critical because a child's integrity is in question, and the parent's integrity may be questioned by the child. Both parent and child deserve respect, not brush-offs. This section includes food for thought about types of thinking, and grants permission to be skeptical.

Many parents ask me whether or not their child is imagining the ghost, implying the ghost must not be real. And many parents ask if they "have to" or are "supposed to" believe in ghosts for the sake of their child.

I wish black-and-white answers were readily available, but every parent's culture, values, religions, views about spiritual life, and thinking styles influence those answers. For a onetime ghost event, it probably is not necessary that parents believe in ghosts. However, when the child has imaginary friends and continues to communicate with these friends in puberty and into the teen years, then a parent and child need to make discussion time about realities, worldviews, agreements, and disagreements.

In this book, you'll read several times that the professionals and psychics who, like me, work with children who see ghosts ask parents to

1. Listen to their children.

2. Don't dismiss them or put them down.

3. Ask questions.

4. Observe how the child interacts with the spirit, and understand any life circumstances that might be influencing the child's perceptions.

When parents have the information they need, they feel more confident in helping a child overcome fear and put any event into perspective. Those four steps help the child stay connected to the parent's heart and allow him or her the time and opportunity for further exploration and understanding. Don't think that you can shield children from fear or feel that you have to take care of all their fears. Kids learn resilience just like parents learned it by gaining life experience with confidence in knowing mom or dad support them.

The minimum attitude a parent could offer for a child who sees ghosts would be one of possibility: "Maybe you do see something." The moderate attitude would be, "Let's explore and learn together." A breast cancer survivor shared her mental focus with me as she was going through treatment, and I think it is applicable here. Each day, she said to herself: "It is what it is." This means she focused precisely on each event of that day, whether it was making a sandwich or having chemotherapy.

Whether your child refuses to go into his or her bedroom because a ghost lives there, sees the spirit of Uncle Lou in the corner of garage, or talks to an angel, it is what it is! Whether or not you believe in ghosts or feel your child is playing a game, it is still what it is. That attitude keeps you focused on the event and your child, and keeps you from spinning into fears or fatigue. How do you think a child experiences fear?

When we suggest a parent believe, we mean to believe in the child—to believe that the child believes!

—CARON GOODE

How Children Experience Fear

For those children who are really afraid, the visceral feelings in the abdomen may cramp or squeeze so tightly that the children may lose their ability to speak. Their thinking freezes up and their minds may go blank, unable to process the concept of "ghost." Remember, the body has the experience first, and the mind understands the experience later. Some children experience fear of ghosts as a shock, and need some recovery time.

So asking questions is not helpful in the beginning, and can be more confusing if a parent is pressing for information when the child's mental pilot light goes out. Disoriented children need gentle touch, soft reassurances, and, if necessary, removal from the environment with the ghosts until they are ready to talk about it or face it. Children's first priority is feeling safe and secure. The parent's first priority needs to match if positive results are to come.

Another aspect of children's interactions with spirit walkers is a "feeling" in the room or atmosphere. When I met the friar ghost in Peru, I felt a distinct chill in the room. Children may feel chills up their spine, get goose bumps, feel cold or hot spots in the environment, or intuitively feel guided to move to another space.

How Parents Respond to Fear

Fears are a natural part of growing up. During the preschool years, children often fear animals, dark, imaginary creatures, and natural events like storms, fires, thunder, and lightning. Parents who criticize a child for his fears, who are sarcastic, or even punish a child for having fears, are not helping to reduce the fears.
—STEPHEN J. BEVELED

The following general guidelines on fear will help parents as they help their children face their fears of spirit walkers, regardless of whether or not the parents believe their child has actually seen something. Belief isn't necessary, but awareness or openness are, because we usually don't think through these fear situations with our children so much as respond from our own visceral feelings!

- Fear is a healthy response and adaptive behavior to any perceived danger.

- Few children have all the skills to learn to shift out of fear. Parents are the ones who model, role-play, and act out these skills for helping children handle fears.

- Fear is best met with confidence, a sense of empowerment that enables one to face fear, or a feeling that one is brave enough to deal with the situation even if fearful.

- Parents will observe that a child's fear responses are immediate and consistent. Most children respond to stress or fear in a predictable way based upon their core temperament.

- Doers want the parent to "do" something about the fear or show them how to deal with it. Doers like to push through, persevere, use trial and error approaches until something works. They often persist until worn out.

- Thinkers are shy of fearful situations and need more information before choosing how to live with or deal with things. They prefer to back away until mentally comfortable. These children would enjoy online research, storybooks about ghosts, talking with a mentor, and such. Don't get lost in the gathering information stage. Instead use the information to make informed choices.

- Children who are peacekeepers like harmony in their environment and in relationships, and may back away from scary situations at first. However, with help, they can gain confidence when you help them solve their fears by asking questions, playing "what if" mental scenarios, pretending and imagining solutions until one feels right to the child.

- Intuitive, creative children have heightened feelings about the situation. You can't deny their feelings, push them aside or talk them away. A child's solutions comes from "feeling into" the situation based upon the child's internal sense: feeling how to move away from the ghost, feeling how to create a door of light for the ghost to go home, knowing how to create a "space" for the spirit walker within the home.

- Do you get the idea that each temperament has a different way of dealing with fears? If not addressed, fear can become anxiety and escalate into a phobia. Doers can become riddled with anxiety and get confused and tired. Thinkers can mentally box themselves into denial and hide in seeking-more-info behavior while the angst simmers beneath the surface. Peacemakers or harmonizers want to adapt, to fix it, to make all feel better, even helping the ghost. Not being in harmony creates the anxiety and they want to help. Intuitive feelers seek to solve any issue through a feeling sense, expressing in art, using creativity, connecting with the ghost.

- If not addressed, chronic fear can cause health issues by weakening the immune system.

Parents who are fearful of ghosts are afraid for their children as well as themselves. Cautious and concerned parents worry for their children's fears and will educate themselves on how to handle the situation. Parents like Doreen Fisher (see section two) accept their children's ability to see spirit walkers and spirit animals as part of their lifestyle and stay aware of how to deal with the day-to-day situations that arise.

In summary, kids seeing ghosts may be new territory for child and parent. Parents may have to make up the parenting role as they go along if they have no previous experience with the spirit world. Or as one parent said to me, "My kid seeing ghosts is so far out of my league, a solution of giving the boy a pill would be a lot easier. But I've never taken the easy way out with my boy. If you tell me I have to stretch my brain, then I'll do that." This mom represents the type of mind-set that Dr. Robert Flower calls exceptional thinking, being open to possibility.

In my experience with intuitive children throughout the last twenty years, I have found that certain thinking styles either help us empower our children or limit our ability to help them. I turned to Robert Flower, an expert in the science of human achievement, to respond to my question of how parents can identify their thinking style, and learn to shift thinking to stay open and receptive to ghosts.

Your exceptional mind can cure the fears that affect you.

—ROBERT FLOWER

Robert Flower Explains How Using Exceptional Thinking Can Break Through Fears

Director and founder of the Gilchrist Institute *(www.gilchristforum .com)*, Robert Flower is a graduate of Fordham University and Walden University. He holds a Ph.D. in organizational and human-system sciences. A Mensa scholar and sports enthusiast, he developed a sports and mind enhancement program, which was based upon his discovery of natural intelligences. He later applied his work on natural intelligences to the field of the achievement sciences, then, ultimately, to the secret of exceptional thinking.

I asked Flower to condense his thirty years of research into the sciences of learning and achievement to discuss how our thinking limits or improves our ability to help children handle their fears. If there is a certain mind-set or specific manner of thinking that would enhance our skills, don't we want to know?

I chose to include two of Robert's experiences with ghosts to show how he helped other people deal with their fears, especially through the use of an oscillating sound machine.

FLOWER'S PERSONAL EXPERIENCES

I've had several experiences with ghosts. One experience was with a very good friend of mine a number of years ago. He was sitting in his home, watching television. He suddenly turned around, looked down the hallway, and saw a man. The man looked at him, started to walk toward him, and then made a right turn into the wall.

My friend had no idea what that was all about, and this happened to him twice. He told me about it after the second time, mostly out of fear, because he thought the house was haunted. I told him to get an oscillating sound machine that he could flip on and off whenever he wanted, because I'm definitely of the opinion that everything is a frequency and a vibration. By setting the oscillator to specific frequencies, he could either call the ghosts or dissipate them with vibration, with energy signals. My friend never had another problem in his home after that.

Another incident was with a woman who had all kinds of ghostly apparitions and poltergeist occurrences in her apartment. Objects went flying all over the place—from pots and pans to pens and pencils.

I went there with my friend, who had asked me to assist the woman. I didn't see any ghosts, although the three of us felt that there definitely was something in the house. I was able to make it disappear by eliminating fear and generating confidence within the other two people and myself. The woman never had another problem.

The three of us generated positive power feelings throughout the apartment. In other words, I was the source of positive power in the room, and they needed to be with me to generate a strong positive energy in the house, because if they weren't with me, the apparition had a host—the woman—whose energy attracted the spirit. By changing the feeling dynamics in the room, so changed the environment.

So we needed all of us to be in control of the emotions we were emitting throughout the house and overcome our fears so that there wouldn't be any further affective results. I suspect the fears of the woman attracted the ghostly activity in the first place.

I have had some very positive experiences also. For instance, when we were buying our current house, we were in this very old house, looking at this wreck, trying to decide whether we were going to buy it.

I came to the living room and placed my hand against the door buck, and all of a sudden, I felt tremendous heat coming out of the wooden doorjamb. I couldn't figure that out. Then I started to get this vibration, like a repeating, electrical impulse in the stomach. I've never experienced anything like it before or after, but that's the best way I can describe it. I knew intuitively that somebody was signaling me that this was a place where I had to be.

This was such a strange occurrence that we ended up buying this house, and we've been here ever since. I never thought that I would have bought it because of the price, the condition of the place, and other factors. In addition, I was under contract to buy another house. So I ended up getting out of that other contract, buying this home, and everything has worked out super since.

What is the common ground, so to speak, of all these stories? That there is an underlying reality that is more powerful than our everyday reality, and we're not paying attention to it. We can influence this underlying reality through our emotionality and through our focus. Also how we think heavily influences what we see and what we are open to in our worldviews.

WHY DO WE NOT PAY ATTENTION
TO THE UNDERLYING REALITY?

The reason we do not pay attention to the underlying reality is because of our limiting thinking and where we focus in our daily tasks. Most of us, in our day-to-day living, operate in one or two levels of thinking—called *automatic thinking* and *institutional thinking*—because our environments demand these types of thinking in how we operate. Few of us call on inspiration or creative thinking skills, so we miss those moments of creativity with children. Yet it is precisely the more exceptional and creative thinking that we need for children who see ghosts, in order to inspire their confidence in dealing with their fears.

Let's review each level so you can identify your current thinking and where you can grow and stretch in order to be open-minded and help your children.

Automatic thinking is the state in which we normally operate, with little, if any, thought whatsoever. At this level, our thinking is habitual or robotic, because we don't need to be creative or aware. We dress, bathe, drive, answer phones or questions, and even handle the kids or coworkers without much planning, foresight, or interaction. We conduct most of our work on automatic. We are unaware of creativity and of a larger perspective.

Institutional thinking can be described as the arena where our environment and relationships dictate how we think, choose, and act. We behave as we were taught, and we adapt to others from preconceived rules. How we relate, adapt, or understand our environment and people within it stems from the stronger social and cultural influences of family, religion, education, politics, governmental regulations, and corporate dictates. Sometimes, this level of thinking is like a closed loop, causing us to respond to children with colloquial comments like, "You're making that

AUTOMATIC THINKING	INSTITUTIONAL THINKING	EXCEPTIONAL THINKING
If I know something you don't, I'm smarter.	If I know someone famous, I'm better than others.	My strength comes from knowledge and understanding.
Money makes me a better person.	Some people think they hit a triple just because they were born on third base.	Overcoming my weaknesses makes me better.
By dropping names, I'm important.	I'm unique and therefore better than others.	My significance is in my inner strength.
I'm inclined toward discussions about others and myself.	Where I live, work, and socialize defines my worth.	I'm inclined toward discussions of ideas and ideals.
I have little time for or interest in reading.	I'm inclined toward discussions concerning places and events.	I'm a truth seeker.
You can't beat city hall.	I read biographies and novels.	Democracy requires "eternal vigilance."
Money solves all problems.	Trying to beat city hall is not worth the effort.	Problems are gateways to excellence.
This is how it is!	Money and whom you know solves problems.	I'm a researcher; I seek absolutes.
Just my luck.	My mind is made up; don't confuse me with facts.	Luck prefers the prepared mind.
I say what's on my mind.	It's not meant to be for me.	I express truth with compassion and sensitivity.
	I say what is politically correct.	

up. That's stupid. You must be evil." Get the idea? No room for an opening, or even for conversation or questions, with a child, because our rigidity or worldview can't see it or know it.

With *exceptional thinking*, we synthesize issues, think through actions, and base decisions on facts or evidence—not opinion, hearsay, emotion, or preferences. Exceptional thinking rejects and rises above limitations of ego, fear, ignorance, and self-deception, which lead us to express negative emotionality or irrationality.

Proactive-type thinking easily synthesizes people, cultures, and beliefs. Within exceptional thinking is the ability to choose options, to be creative in empowering children through fears, and to be free of judgments. This is the kind of thinking we want to bring to any ghostly situations, and we want to share examples of such thinking with our kids. Let's face it—our kids need creative solutions, not our opinions or put-downs.

We may function at one level, two, or even three levels throughout our lives. Each stage of human development brings challenges, which stretch our learning and require different thinking skills. Review the chart to the left with sample quips from each thinking level, and find yourself.

I hope the examples show you how exceptional thinking empowers you to handle some of these situations our children face. The unknown is a new frontier and involves our children's fragile psyches. What would exceptional thinking by a parent look like when they're handling these kinds of ghostly apparitions with their children?

First, use exceptional thinking to reject your limitations. The four limitations of fear, ignorance, ego, and self-deception keep you from learning new strategies to help your children.

Fear freezes you so you, with your child, are afraid of ghosts. Huddled together, you face the unknown without a solution because fear means you think someone or something can hurt you.

When we personalize fear, it rules us. An exceptional-thinking approach is to face fear and conquer your limitation.

Ignorance means lack of information. If you do not have enough information to deal with a ghostly situation, then it is time to find someone who can help, or find a book or Internet information on the topic, such as the website "Intuitive Parenting for Intuitive Kids" *(http://intuitiveparenting.wordpress.com)*. Exceptional thinking says educate yourself, find out strategies, and ask for help or support.

Ego is our sense of self-identity, which influences how we accept new situations. Ego limits us when we lose touch with our awareness and live mostly in the robotic thinking. We cannot create solutions or brainstorm ideas with our kids or find new ways to tell the story and laugh our way to facing fear. An inflated-type ego comes across more like a bragging teen than a concerned parent whose kid needs answers. The way to shift out of ego in order to help your child is to see the world through their eyes, feel their fear, and ask questions: *How can I help? What do you need? May I hold you? Can you answer a few questions?*

Self-deception is one result of the first three limitations, when we fall into the unproductive practice of believing that a false idea, feeling, or situation is true, like "Ghosts don't exist"; "You, child, are lying"; or "Don't bother me, kid, I am watching television." Self-deception allows us to close our eyes to other realities that intersect our world and that we cannot understand or deny.

In essence, we are hardwired genetically to feel and experience these great restrictors. Throughout human evolution, for example, fear served its purpose as a warning system for environmental dangers. So evolution has worked for us and against us. Unfortunately, the limitations are the antithesis to exceptional thinking. In our modern world, the restrictors or limitations make us products of rote thinking and limited potential—very limited.

In summary, the limitations keep us below the radar of awareness, fortify false beliefs, and poorly communicate our intent to be exceptional!

If you care for your child's best welfare and a healthy mental framework and an expansion of their intelligence, you adopt an accepting environment rather than a rejecting environment.

Seek the positive aspects of fear and self-deception that teach you a new way to approach the situation. The four restrictors present opportunities for learning. To help a child feel empowered, you have to stand simply in your power, creating an environment of power that says, "I am in control, fear or no fear. I stand strong." Your reality is the correct reality.

Let me postulate it like this: If one has a bout with cancer, and it happens only once in one's life, it is not a typical reality. But it is a reality, and you have to deal with it.

The Skeptic's View from Joe Nickell

This section presents the skeptic's viewpoint. I have asked Joe Nickell, Ph.D., to speak his mind on the topic of ghosts, entities, and energies in order to provide you with a well-rounded discussion.

Nickell *(www.joenickell.com)* is the "modern Sherlock Holmes," employed as the only full-time professional paranormal investigator. Over the last forty years he has investigated historical documents, relics, and paranormal events and has authored twenty-five books on the topics of his investigations. His professional experiences as a private investigator, and also as a magician and mentalist, led him to explore the Shroud of Turin as well as famous hauntings. He explains that mysteries should neither be fostered nor dismissed, but carefully investigated so that answers can be found.

PSEUDOSCIENCE

Ghosts are a popular belief in survival of the human spirit or life force. Most people who believe in ghosts conceive of some sort of energy that survives death. The problem with that is that that's not a scientific concept. "Energy" makes it sound like science, but they're not defining energy in a way that science would define energy, because they're defining something that doesn't behave like energy.

Any ability of the brain to continue to produce some force after one is dead, or for such a force to have the ability to think without an organ such as the brain, is pretty much scientific nonsense. Any kind of energy that the body would give off would dissipate once the source for the energy is terminated. So we're not really talking about energy.

People talk about ghosts as a mystical, magical force, not energy. We have a name for that which sounds superficially like science, but fundamentally isn't science. The name is "pseudoscience." So any claims that one is somehow showing evidence of the life energy is false. Ghost hunters who go through supposedly haunted places with electromagnetic field meters and other gadgetry claiming that they're somehow picking up ghostly energy are engaging in classic pseudoscience. They don't know what they're doing. These people are not scientists. They're using scientific instruments to be sure, but they're not proceeding in a scientific manner, and any effect that the meter shows, the least likely explanation for it would be that it's a ghost.

The scientific evidence for ghosts is nonexistent, and it's not for the skeptic to prove that ghosts don't exist. The burden of proof, as one knows from a court of law and from the court of science and scholarship, is on the advocate of an idea. So it's true that one can't prove there are no ghosts, just as one cannot prove there are no leprechauns in Ireland. But one, fortunately, does not have that burden.

GHOST HUNTING ON THE FRINGE

Ghost hunting is in the fringe area. The British ghost hunter who probably was the first person who coined the term "ghost hunter" was Harry Price, who had a ghost-hunting kit and investigated Borley Rectory in England. He famously became the first prominent ghost hunter. Then in America, Hans Holzer was the dean of ghost hunters throughout the second half of the twentieth century from about 1950, until his recent death [2009]. He said that this ghost-hunting business with gadgetry was "utter nonsense."

WAKING DREAMS AND SLEEP PARALYSIS

It's fascinating that we human beings see ghosts. The question is under what conditions do we see ghosts? When we look at claims of ghost sightings, there are some things that I've found in my forty years of observation. Quite a number of the sightings occur when someone is lying in bed. There are numerous cases in which the person says, "I woke up, and I saw a ghostly form standing by my bed, walking through the wall, leaning over," or what have you.

My first ghost case was McKenzie House in Toronto, Canada, and a caretaker's wife had reported a ghostly figure. She awoke to see a ghostly figure leaning over her bed. Now this is what is known as a "waking dream." This is a well-understood phenomenon—understood alike by my associates who are psychologists and those who are neurologists, who study the brain.

We know that these experiences are a type of hallucination, and they're divided generally into two types:

• Hypnagogic, which occur when you're going to sleep,

• Hypnopompic, which occur when you're waking up.

It is useful to understand the difference between the two types. If you're just going to sleep, you may not reach that deepest state in which your body completely shuts down. When you've been fully asleep and wake out of that state, you may have sleep paralysis, a condition in which the person waking up feels paralyzed and is unable to move, but is conscious of being awake and seeing what's going on.

What's interesting is that this is a physiological thing happening to the person—this waking up and being in a state between fully awake and fully asleep, particularly experiencing the paralysis, hallucinating, and seeing strange, maybe terrifying things. We can trace that phenomenon back through history. We know that people experienced this in the Middle Ages. They had demons called incubi and succubae come to them in the night and sit on them and hold them down; hence the paralysis. We know that in the Victorian era people saw gray ladies' ghosts and often were "paralyzed" with fear. We especially know now, with the development of this exciting modern mythology of alien visitations, that people wake up to find themselves strapped down and aliens arrayed around them: small, big-eyed, big-headed humanoids apparently ready to do some horrible surgical procedure on them.

We're dealing with the same phenomenon—this waking dream with sleep paralysis being interpreted due to the cultural and psychological concepts of the time. So people are having the same physiological experience, but it's being interpreted differently. And their hallucinatory experience is taking a different form due to their cultural expectations. I have noticed that people who wake up in a haunted house are more apt to see a ghost. They don't see aliens. Describing this waking-dream experience similarly, people who have read Whitley Strieber's book *Communion* wake up to see aliens.

In summary: These are powerful experiences. We've learned these are fairly well-understood experiences, and they are essentially physiological. They are triggered by some little glitch in brain activity—maybe something to do with poor sleeping patterns.

STATES OF MIND

The content of these experiences is psychological and cultural, so they stem from our hopes and/or our fears. I think that our state of mind comes into play when we see things that aren't there, or we misperceive it (think it's a monster like Bigfoot), or we have some waking-dream experience. Sometimes we cast these mysterious, paranormal entities as fearful creatures, bogeymen, and aliens coming to do something terrible to us. Bigfoot might be a monster that will carry us away. Demons might do something awful to us. All these are simply expressions of our fears coming out and making these perceptions into bogeymen.

At the same time, other people might perceive the same set of entities as quite hopeful. One woman I interviewed told me about waking up and seeing the ghost of her dead father at a time when she was having some struggles in her life, and he assured her that everything would be all right. This was a powerful, moving, and hopeful experience. There was nothing terrifying about it. This ghost was her father, and she got a comforting message. Again, other people claim to have contact with aliens that give them messages about coming for the planet Earth.

Human beings are both rational and emotional creatures. We can think with the organ above the neck, but a lot of times we think with our emotions. The organs below the neck move us: the heart and the gut. So the paranormal, quite often in ghost experiences, catches us thinking with our emotions. They go directly to the heart or directly to our hopes and fears. They tap our emotions, and then our organ above the neck, our brain, kicks in to explain what's happened. The powerful emotional effect trumps the brain's effect. In other words, we may basically not believe in ghosts or know that ghosts don't exist. Yet when we have a visitation from our dead father, it's another matter. That emotional power is so great that it may push aside our reasoning ability to realize that what we actually had was a dream.

DREAMLIKE STATES

Apparitional sightings tend to appear in that dreamlike state. They don't happen, in other words, when one is doing something intense and one's concentration is taken by the activity. You're focusing carefully while you're operating a buzz saw. That's not when the ghosts happen.

They happen when you're laid-back. And a lot of times people are not in bed. They're sitting on the sofa watching TV; they don't realize that they've drifted into a dreamlike state, but you'll find that a lot of times people are relaxed.

People typically say, "I thought I saw something out of the corner of my eye." That's a common little perceptive trick that you perceive movement out of the corner of your eye. When they turn, they say they see a ghostly figure briefly, and almost always as soon as they look at it, it disappears.

From my experience, and this is well supported by science, what's happening in these cases is that one is having a welling up from the subconscious. Perhaps because of where they are, something in the back of their mind momentarily flashes up. They are in Gettysburg, let's say, and they may not have been consciously thinking about Civil War soldiers. However, because of the general ambience and history, they perceive a movement. They turn and think they saw a Civil War soldier, maybe. It fades immediately, and they say, "Okay, so I saw a ghost."

What actually happened is that the images from the subconscious have welled up momentarily and superimposed themselves on the visual scene, almost in the same way that a camera can have a double exposure. Your actual sight images are happening in the brain, and that's the source of the mental image as well. So the two become momentarily confused. One imagines something, and at the same time superimposes it on the outer world. So these are not actually sightings of something out there, but are again apparitional experiences not unlike waking dreams.

PHOTOGRAPHS OF GHOSTS

Then, of course, we have the evidence that people photograph ghosts. It is rare that someone sees a ghost and then photographs it. In some famous cases when that's happened, it's actually all a hoax. A person claims to have seen a ghost, and they can show that the ghost figure on the stairs is, in fact, a faked photograph. Most often what people will say is this: "You know, we didn't see anything, but we took some pictures. We didn't know until we had our photographs processed that there was anything there.

But here are our pictures, and look, we have ghostly orbs. We have funny spiraling strands and strands streaking across the photograph."

These are often interpreted as ghost orbs of "spirit energy," or the strands may be interpreted as ectoplasmic forces. In most cases, the orbs are particles of dust or occasionally fine droplets of moisture in the air bouncing back the flash. They look like big balls of light out in the room, but that's not what happened. The flash went off, and a tiny speck, just a tiny distance away from the camera lens usually, has bounced back the flash and produced this bright orb. The strands are quite often the wrist strap, or the camera strap has gotten in front of the lens. I may have been the first to recognize and write about that phenomenon many years ago. At that time, it was unknown to me, and I puzzled it out on my own.

So the camera-strap effect is well-known, and the orb effect is well-known. Some more sensible ghost hunters have learned to disavow those phenomena, but some say, "Oh yes, well of course some orbs are dust particles, but we've photographed some orbs we think are actually real ghost energy." This is usually coming from the same kind of ghost-hunting amateurs who don't know what they're doing and is not evidence of anything.

The earliest spirit photographs began in Boston in the 1860s with a man named William Mumler, who was actually making a type of double exposure using glass-plate negatives. When you look at photographs prior to glass plates—tintypes and before that, the daguerreotypes—there were no ghosts. When glass-plate negatives came to the fore and made double exposures possible, you started getting fake spirit pictures. Eventually with cameras being put in the hands of ordinary folk, various camera glitches started showing up, and people would interpret a blur or something odd in a photograph to being a ghost.

I think it's safe to say that mainstream science has not authenticated a single ghost photo—not one—although there are, of course, countless claimants for the title. So I think, as much as we would like to visualize ghosts, they remain the subject of our mental state.

ALWAYS TWO SIDES

What we have quite often in the world of the paranormal are two groups, characterized as believers and disbelievers, talking about, "Do you believe this?" "No, I don't believe it." Over and over again, they use the word "belief," *when science is not about belief at all.* They ought not to be saying, "Well, I believe in ghosts, and I've heard footsteps on the stairs, and that confirms it. That's enough for me." That's the wrong approach. Or someone says, "I don't believe in ghosts; it's nonsense and can't happen." I think those two approaches are wrong because the issues and the consequences are important.

If we survived death, we would want to know that. There's hardly anything one can think of more crucial than that. So we ought not have a dogma about it. I'm quick to state that it's very unlikely that ghosts exist and science can't justify how a ghost could exist and be able to think and have motor activity without a brain. This all seems very, very unlikely. Nevertheless, what I'm saying is, "Look, sincere, intelligent, brilliant people—honest people, not idiots, hoaxers, and crazy people, but quite decent, intelligent people—are experiencing ghostly phenomena."

It behooves us to determine what is happening. Maybe it's not a ghost, but if people are concerned, then I'm concerned. If great numbers of people are concerned over this issue, then I want to know what's going on. Rather than start with an answer, I free my thinking up at the door.

Coleridge called the "willing suspension of disbelief" the right attitude to have. I may say, "My belief or lack of belief is just not relevant now. I'm on the prowl looking for the truth." I want to have something happen. I want to figure out why it's happening, and I'm confident that if I can find an explanation, as at McKenzie House with the footsteps on the stairs or the waking-dream apparition, any needed debunking will take care of itself. So I am honestly looking for evidence and think this is a valid topic to look into. I think we ought not to have an agenda of what to believe until we've gotten to the site, found out precisely what the claim is, and then tried to explain it.

Talking to Kids

At some point you might want to tell kids that there's no evidence that ghosts are a reality. It's well and good to humor a child and say, "I respect you. I know you've had an experience. You've woken up, and you've seen something." But you don't serve people well, I think, when you deceive them. When you say, "Okay, this wasn't a real weeping icon, but it's okay to tell a little lie for Jesus. We'll fake the weeping icon because so many people love to come and believe they've seen a miracle. So they'll line up, and we'll renew the faith, and what harm can be done?" Well, one of the harms is that you've lied, and you've perpetrated a sort of idolatry of the icon. I would not recommend telling the child, "Yes, it's a ghost, but it won't hurt you." Now I would go further and say, "We have no evidence that ghosts exist other than in our minds. They can seem very real to us under certain conditions," and then, try to explain those conditions. I think that would be helpful.

Empowering Children

*Authentic empowerment is knowing that you
are on purpose, doing God's work, peacefully and
harmoniously.*

—WAYNE DYER

Empowerment is the ability to take action. We empower our children through our communication, both verbal and nonverbal. When we teach them self-reliance, they learn persistence and develop resilience that expresses as self-confidence when children have acquired enough information about their environment that they feel confident in interacting with it.

Five-year-old Jason expressed empowerment when he put on his pirate's hat, his black eye patch, and dauntingly shook his sword toward his bedroom closet, daring the ghost in there to leave. "Hardy har, me ghosty. Leave now, I say, and go someplace else. Or I'll make ya walk the plank and you'll sink to the bottom of the sea. All the big sharks will eat you." The empowerment game worked. Jason slept in his bed that night, and did not see the ghost again.

Our goal is to help our children transform fears into empowered feelings, thoughts, and actions. Fear is a healthy response, but prolonged or sudden fear can cause children undue distress and anxiety. Children who are frightened become reactive, rather than responsive, to their environment. Habitual reactions can escalate into fear patterns and chronic stress, no matter what the child's age. The ultimate fear, of course, would become the ghost in the room, an invasion of a child's private space involving a different, unfamiliar world. Don't we want our children to be able to manage this fear of the unknown?

In my book *Nurture Your Child's Gift* (Beyond Words, 2008), contributor and author Joy Watson defined empowerment as:

Will + belief in self = the ability to act or take action

Watson also explained that empowerment is not something anyone can give a child. Rather, a child feels empowered by having experiences in which they learn how to successfully influence or control their environment. Sequential, successful steps are the answer to helping children manage fears.

Coping Skills

Researchers have concluded that how children cope under stress in the present tells us whether or not they will become more secure adults. Research shows that certain emotional responses like optimism, empathy, confidence, and the ability to observe a situation empowers people to deal more effectively with stressful events. Flexibility is also an excellent coping skill because we do not always have control of the event that causes stress.

In addition, being able to accept a situation is a better coping skill than helplessness or depression. Coping skills tend to fall into two categories and depend upon whether a person can actively engage in the situation or not.

1. Actively engaging is facing the situation, observing it, gathering information, seeking answers, generating possibilities, or seeking support.

2. If a child cannot actively engage, then coping includes escapism, avoidance, wishing things were different, denial, or the use of distractions to remove one's self from the situation. This grouping can help any child or adult deal with the initial fears.

The ideal scenario would be for the parent to then empower a child with the strategies listed in this section to face or walk through the fear.

Our goal for empowering children is to transform stress and fear into feelings of safety by introducing coping skills like humor and play. Using touch coupled with empathy is a strong tool to calm a child immediately and reminding them that they are safe.

Touch

Touch and empathy have a profound effect on a child's right brain as well as the limbic system, cerebellum, and the autonomic nervous system, all of which are involved in processing social and emotional interactions. They also govern states of stress and relaxation and helps determine the child's ability to cope actively or passively with a stress or fear.

By touching a child in a way that is comforting, you stimulate his or her internal soothing response. By pairing touch with empathy, that is, receiving the child without attempts to impose a perspective, a parent shows the child how to accept himself and calm his nervous system.

Acupressure

Acupressure is one form of traditional Chinese medicine that involves placing gentle pressure with your fingers or hand on different acupuncture points. Acupressure touch is a gentle, focused contact directly on the given point. Points where a gentle pressure touch is helpful include:

1. On either side of the neck vertebrae, at the base of the neck, above the shoulder curvature

2. On top of the shoulder line, about half way from the neckline, in the indentation of the joint.

3. The center of the inside of the elbow.

4. On the temples.

5. In the center of the top of the head.

6. In the web of skin between the thumb and forefinger.

The importance of touch continues throughout one's life. Why is this true? In the developing embryo, a primitive layer of cells called the ectoderm produces both the skin and the nervous system. Touch is the concrete anatomical and physiological connection that provides "food" to the nervous system that allows the human being to experience that it exists. Touch and movement provide the stimulus that regulates and supports physiological processes.

Play to Integrate the Scary Emotions

Play is the language of children. Playing for children is like talking for adults. Play is the most natural self-expression for children of all ages. An adult communicating with a child during play is a highly effective way to facilitate managing fear and moving through stress. Think of children's emotions, as "energy in motion." Our language about emotions reflects when feelings are stuck, knotted up, or clogged. Stuck feelings need expression, and we give our children the opportunity to express through playing and verbalizing with them, even asking leading questions to help them solve their own ghost dilemma.

Play provides a nonthreatening environment for children to reveal thoughts and feelings. Replaying activities like seeing the ghost, running out of the room to a parents' bedroom can be reenacted to defuse the reactive fear of the ghost. The next day, continue reenacting the game in the daytime, and this time, include a solution to managing the ghost.

For example, Lindsey would not sleep in her bedroom after she announced that she had seen a "tall, skinny woman" staring at her in her bed. Once she left her bedroom, she forgot that she had not retrieved her bunny that was also in the bed. Lindsey was sure the bunny was scared too. Lindsey's parents retrieved the bunny and allowed her to sleep on the couch that night. However, the next day they engaged Lindsey in a replay of the scene, and this time after several productions, Lindsey retrieved the bunny herself, and then stayed in her room with her bunny and asked questions of the tall female ghost. When Lindsey returned to her bedroom that night, so did the ghost. Lindsey got her parents, and the three of them sat on Lindsey's bed, and she directed her parents where to stare although they did not see Lindsey's ghost in the corner.

Lindsey's mom started to feel like her grandmother was in the room. She retrieved a picture of her grandmom from a box of family pictures and showed Lindsey. Mom asked the ghost, "Pearl, is that you?" Lindsey nodded yes in response to the tall thin woman's nod.

Lindsey's playing and replaying through the scary part and finding a solution gave her active control of the situation. She was able to assimilate the emotions of the ghost event in a positive way.

Playing is an innate need for children and allows them to explore and master their environment in daily life. As linear thinking develops, imagination takes on a more important role in children's lives. Children use their imagination when they read, write in a diary, daydream, doodle, draw or paint, play store or school, play fantasy games on the computer or role-play new social skills. Playing and using the imagination facilitate children's confidence as they learn to be competent in a fearful environment. The pleasure of play neutralizes fear. Pretending and playing is one world where children have control—a space where they can invite the ghost at will, converse with, or ask the ghost to leave.

Talking It Through

This approach is especially helpful for children older than ten or whose reasoning skills are developed. Most parents use conversation for talking about the normal anxieties and fears of childhood, and in this book, those interviewed have consistently said, "listen, listen," when children bring up seeing ghosts. Listening rather than talking is critical for communication.

When using the method of talking it through for ghost-related incidents, parents are looking for solutions, but also for the relationship of the incident to the child's thoughts and feelings. Parents can use the child's thoughts to guide the emotional behavior and establish solutions, identifying a relationship between seeing the ghost and feelings.

Talk it through to educate a child that he or she is in charge of the environment. First identify scary feeling in order to objectify what is inside: Name a feeling you feel. Where is it in your body? How heavy is it? What color is it? Can you draw it and describe it to me?

Correlate the feelings and thoughts to the ghost encounter: Did the feelings trigger any scary thoughts? Did you imagine any scenes in your head? Did your mind go blank? Did you want to run and do something else? Describe what you thought or how your thoughts flowed.

Discern required action through open-ended questions: When I train parent coaches to help parents and children communicate better regarding any issue, first we gauge willingness and readiness—then agreement. If a child is not ready, willing, or able to commit to action, then as parents we must wait for the child to feel comfortable. We ask: Are you willing? Are you able? Can you act now? Will you make a commitment to follow through? Ready to roll?

There is a good reason for using those words like ready, willing, and able. Helping children to gain cognitive mastery—thinking they are ready, and then willing—prepares them emotionally. They are affirming the parent and reassuring themselves. So, keep checking in verbally to get a handle on your child's emotional preparedness.

Self-Affirmation

Positive self-talk statements must be adapted to the child's age and made into simple statements of affirming qualities or actions. (I am brave. I can go into my bedroom.) Statements can contain a thought of self-reward. (I handled that well. I did a great job.) Usually children need help from parents in making the rewarding statements because they believe those statements when they are validated or affirmed by the parent. They learn the positive value of the thought when the parents reflect that positive value.

The cognitive aspects of positive statements help a child think through actions and change fearful thoughts to affirming thoughts. They open the imagination for children to create solution-oriented or action-oriented scenarios.

Using Books and Stories

Reading self-help books with children helps them see how a character copes with a ghost. The focus is on modeling a child's reaction to the ghost situation and uses the story to personalize it to a child's situation. Parents can encourage further solutions in storytelling, as in, "Let's retell that story with you as the main character," "Can you tell me a similar story about you and your ghost just like the storybook character," or "How do you think that child in the book handled it? Does it give you some ideas?"

Making your own storybook about the ghost is writing a new script. Write out the scene as if it is a play being performed on a stage and the child or teen is the main character. Describe the stage in detail. Entering stage right is the main character, and entering stage left is the ghost character. Describe the interaction as it occurs, but leave the ending open for different scenarios.

Here is where family brainstorming can help a child or teen develop inspiring, laughable, and outlandish endings that might dissipate fear. Help children create their own ending and encourage them to transform their fear into an empowered action.

When fourteen-year-old James first saw a cavalry soldier in his bedroom, he thought he was dreaming and went back to sleep. The second time he saw the ghost, James sat up in bed and watched the soldier stare ahead into the distance and walk although he didn't seem to go anywhere. Going back to sleep was not an option for James, and so he woke up his mother to come see the ghost. Of course, she could see nothing. James returned to his bed, but still couldn't sleep. Instead, his mind raced with possibilities—was the soldier lost? Perhaps the soldier never reached his destination and died of thirst in the desert. Maybe Indians or bandits killed him before he reached a fort. Maybe he was walking home after the war. What happened to his horse?

James's thoughts had spun into anxiety by breakfast. His dad suggested they talk through all the possible scenes involving the ghost, and then James could write a play, describing exactly what he saw, how he intuited the soldier's intentions and destinations, and then share that with the family when he was ready.

James did write descriptions of possible endings. His Dad noticed that James's ideas about the cavalry soldier had moved from worrying about him and how he died to helping the solider return home. James didn't see the soldier again, but he learned a very valuable lesson in shifting worry and negative thoughts to more positive perceptions. James reported that this one tool helped him more in his friendships by not thinking the worst of people.

Play and games work well in teaching children personal empowerment. Martial arts is another activity that I often recommend to parents of children who are shy, who don't feel confident among peers, or who are not masterful in their environment. Because the body has an experience first, and the mind understands the experience next in the learning sequence, moving and training the body are very successful ways to help children feel empowered.

Sensei Robert Tallack on Confidence and Character

To address how to empower children, I interviewed a renowned martial arts teacher or sensei, Rob Tallack. He has won three World Traditional Martial Arts Championships and has been teaching children professionally for over thirteen years. In 2007 Robert received his fifth-degree black belt in Goju Ryu karate. He was only twenty-eight at that time, and the promotion required special authorization from Japan because of the minimum age requirements for master grades at fifth-degree black belt.

Tallack's goal is to spread the benefits of martial arts, fitness, and character development to children around the world through the expansion of his company Elementary School Fitness *(www.elementaryschoolfitness.com),* which operates an award-winning program called "Karate Kids" *(www.karatekids.ca).* Tallack is dedicated to providing cost-effective fitness programs to elementary schools worldwide and empowering the development of children's confidence through martial arts.

I chose to interview Robert Tallack because he knows that a consistent step-by-step program of mastering skills does build confidence in fearful, shy, or sensitive children and those who prefer not to participate in team sports. Physical activities for fitness clear out tension, stress, and fear. If parents are not successful in establishing safety and confidence in their kids, then I do recommend a karate program with a compassionate sensei.

CHARACTER BUILDING

In martial arts, the development of empowerment traits like confidence, inner strength, and the ability to avoid peer pressure tend to be the primary focus of children's programs.

Inner strength gives the child the tools and the skills necessary to deal with different fears and different problems. The primary martial-arts strategy for gaining confidence is through movement. For example, when a child comes to a martial-arts center, they may be shy, scared, or being bullied. Typically, the physical symptoms of the conditions are similar, in that the child won't speak much; they're shy and unsure of themselves or have fear issues.

In the martial-arts field, we use physical movement to lead to mental development. We'll get the child running around, doing jumping jacks, and getting physically active. Once their bodies are moving and doing a little bit of exercise, they come out of their shell. Right away, children play games and do some kicks on the heavy bag.

Once the child starts having fun, then their energy or their spirit comes to life, and it works almost exactly the same way every time. What we are able to do is get them physically active, mentally focusing on something that engages their attention, and becoming interactive so they forget their fears.

REDIRECT ATTENTION FROM FEAR WITH
PURPOSEFUL MOVEMENT

The sensei's approach to fearful children is to redirect their attention to purposeful movement. Once a child learns simple movements, he or she can practice the movements when facing fearful situations. A child facing a ghost or any nightly fear can focus and bring awareness to the situation.

> The child's mind is powerful. In a class, when there is an injury like a bumped toe that might cause the child to cry, our protocol is to distract the child and make them start laughing. The instructors are trained to identify the potential injury, and if it's not real, then they make the kids laugh. The instructors ask the child what their favorite type of ice cream is, and as soon as the instructors distract them and their mind focuses, they stop crying. Their body language and their body dynamics completely revert back to being not hurt.
>
> Movement, distraction, and humor are major keys in helping children focus and feel more in control of their bodies and their environments. At the end of the day, a six-year-old child isn't complicated. When you use simple concepts with them like play, movement, and laughter, they respond in kind.

FOCUS AND DISCIPLINE

The sensei continues:

> We move in a different direction once kids are in the dojo and feeling comfortable. The martial-arts industry is unique because it combines modern educational concepts and methods with traditional martial-arts training. In our "Karate Kids" program, for example, we say that martial arts deliver the character-education lessons and concepts.

Historically, the character development associated with traditional martial arts was a by-product of the activity. Let's say fifty years ago, if you went to a karate class in Japan, it was hardcore. In such a formal environment, the values expected were courtesy and respect. You'd go into the dojo, bow to the instructors, and then stand still. You wouldn't move around. You wouldn't speak unless the instructor asked you a question. It was a rigid, formal environment, but the environment created a huge amount of courtesy and respect because the interaction between the students and instructor was mutual. They were bowing to each other, listening to each other. The instructor passed on his knowledge with a great deal of enthusiasm. The students would appreciate it. So the culture created this character development.

When martial arts became more popular in North America and different Asian disciplines made their way to North America, for about a generation or so, the same, traditional, hardcore educational methods from Japan were simply implemented here. In one of the examples from ten or twenty years ago, the martial-arts instructor might walk around the classroom with one of those bamboo swords; he'd whack the students on the legs and say, "Bend your knees lower." Students grimaced with pain, and they were training hard, but they loved the activity. We joke now that there is no way you could get away with walking around a karate class whacking people in the leg with a bamboo stick.

These days, we are using modern educational methods to deliver the same kind of traditional training. Martial arts is a vehicle to help children experience courtesy, respect, focus, and concentration. Under the umbrella of children's confidence, you're getting inner strength, discipline, self-control, awareness, anti-bullying. A self-confident child has the inner strength and the skill set to deal with all of those other issues. The entire structure of a martial-arts program is all about building confidence. Through traditional martial-arts practices, the incremental achievements that the student sees allow them to truly build confidence.

In a good martial-arts center, there's no negativity anymore. For example, it's not, "Hey Johnny, you're doing that front kick wrong. Here's how you do it better." Our instructors are trained to correct a technique by saying, "That's a good front kick, but let's try it this way. Bend your knee a little more forward, keep your hands up higher, and now kick. There you go, that's much better." That language is positive reinforcement and encouragement.

With the instructors, their whole focus in a lesson is getting kids ready for that next progress test. Then, once a month, the students collect a progress stripe on their belt. The belt is a magical tool in martial arts. Kids love their karate belt. The karate belt for a child represents that iconic figure of "the black belt," and they focus on achieving that high level of success.

As soon as they get that white belt, they start collecting these progress stripes on their belts. So to somebody who didn't understand what was happening, the progress stripes would be this fun little reward system for the kids to be collecting. For us, as martial-arts educators, that is one of our most powerful confidence developing tools.

If there's a life skill that needs work, and it doesn't get that work, then the child is missing a block in the foundation for growing up. If they're lacking confidence or self-esteem in their youth, it's only going to amplify and get worse into their teenage years, because that's when anybody's resolve is going to be tested.

We love to work with children between the ages of five and twelve because those are the golden years, where you have an opportunity to lay the foundation for the child to acquire these life skills. If they haven't picked them up by the age of thirteen or so, when they crest into those challenging teenage years, then it's going to be harder for the parents. But if the parent has invested the time in those early years to help the kids develop life skills, then the rest of their life is much easier.

I'll use myself as the example. I grew up doing martial arts, and my parents were both martial-arts educators. I had a pretty positive household. But by the time I was thirteen or fourteen, we moved back from Japan, and my parents separated. I ended up living with my father. I was incredibly fortunate that I had developed a great deal of confidence, self-discipline, and self-control. Growing up through my teenage years, with a single parent who's running a martial-arts center ten hours a day, I had a huge amount of flexibility in my life.

I saw my friends getting into drugs, drinking all the time, and doing things that weren't positive for them. Because I'd grown up doing martial arts in my youth, I understood the concepts of achievement, self-discipline, and self-control.

Tallack emphasizes that children have to have the power to say no and the discernment to say yes at the right tines. The sensitive children, who want to be nice and keep the peace, will cave first to fears, peer pressures, or trying to adapt to others' expectations. They are the first to help spirit people. When, through physical disciplines like karate, kids learn to respect their bodies and treat their bodies with self-respect, they feel empowered to handle most environments.

The sensei continues:

My generation and those before me didn't grow up having these character education lessons. As society has changed, so have the needs for children. So character education is part of the inspiration for the Kids Home Fitness programs. In martial arts, for kids, a lot of their power comes from the "kiai," which means the power yell, that big noise they make. The power within them comes out in the yelling, and the kicks and the punches. We use the energy and excitement around that to help build confidence and power. Next, they get their yellow belt. Now they're feeling cool. They're going to the karate club. Now they're doing sparring and doing some kick and punch drills with partners. Those repetitive empowerment-training exercises truly change the child, and now they feel confident. Essentially, the acquisition of these physical skills leads to mental confidence as well. Physical control leads to mental control. Physical discipline develops mental discipline.

BACK TO SEEING SPIRIT PEOPLE

Let's imagine that we have a child who hasn't been through karate seeing a ghost in the middle of the night. I asked Tallack how he'd suggest a parent might handle that situation, and I like his concept of asking the child for his or her solution before jumping in to fix it for him.

I think in the short term, if somebody came to me and said the child was having that kind of challenge, the first thing I would recommend is that the parent ask the child for the child's solution, if there is one.

Would the simple addition of a night-light help? Does the child need a warm body nearby while he falls asleep? You would be surprised that when we talk to kids, a lot of times they know their own solutions. I remember back in my own childhood when I was living in a three-story house and my bedroom was near the basement. The furnace would turn on in the middle of the night and totally freak me out. When you're seven years old, and this low rumble rattles your room in the night suddenly, it is freaky. If I got freaked out, I would just turn on the night-light and sit up just to see there's no one there.

A lot of times when students lose confidence, or when they're in a situation they're not comfortable with, the first thing to change is their breath. A child who saw a ghost could do a basic breathing exercise: they breathe in, they lift their hands over their head, hold the breath for two seconds, and then they breathe out and bring their hands back down to their own stomach. They'd do this three or four times. It gets their hands up over their heads, which will stretch out their lungs and help them breathe in deeply. And then when they breathe out and bring their hands back down to their stomach, it will help them feel confident, because they're connecting their hands back down to the center of their torso.

The impact of such a simple a breathing exercise is that it controls the person's breath. Most people don't understand how important that is. If you look at any type of an irregular scenario, whether you're scared, nervous, or anxious, your breath is going to go shallow, and your heart rate is going to increase. That is a function of the adrenaline mechanism in your body, when your body shifts to a more adrenalized state, when you breathe more shallowly so your adrenaline is able to release faster if you need to activate the fight or flight mechanism.

So pull a child out of that state by having them breathe in; hold the breath for two or three seconds, which forces the body to relax; and then breathe out while bringing their hands down to the center of the stomach.

A FINAL WORD

The last thing that I would say is that, for children, confidence is the most important life skill they can ever have. Without confidence, it's hard to have anything else, and confidence can be developed in many different ways, such as giving a child something to focus on that allows them to feel like they have a source of power. Once somebody feels that they have that source of power, that sense of power, then they develop a solid foundation to move forward.

I also recommend that all children do martial arts at least for one or two years, because it provides access to character-development training they don't have anywhere else. Any self-defense instructor that is any good knows that a children's self-defense program is 70 percent about the development of self-confidence and 30 percent about the moves.

Terri Jay Endorses Inner Strength and Grounding

Terri Jay, psychic medium and animal communicator *(www.terrijay .com)*, offers hands-on and practical experience in helping parents and children deal with ghosts. Like me, Jay believes in empowering children to take charge of their situations and make choices that strengthen their resolve. I have asked her to share her experience with families and dealing with spirits.

Jay shares:

I think the most important point is to get rid of a lot of the myths about what constitutes ghosts and/or spirits. Basically there's two ways that children see spirits. One is loved ones that have passed away. They know this person although they've never met, like a grandparent. The child will point to a blank wall and say, "Grandpa's there, Grandpa's there." The second way that children see spirits is what I call the negative stuff.

THE NEGATIVE STUFF

What really scares children is the negative stuff, what I would call an entity (defined as a thing with an independent existence).

When we die, we go from being a spiritual being in a physical body to pure spirit. All of our negative experiences, negative thoughts, and negative feelings are shed and left behind in the earth plane.

If the negative vibrations are strong enough, then the negativity can actually coalesce or congeal into an entity. Only the negative earthly experiences are shed. All the happy, positive stuff passes with the person into the higher vibrations of the other side.

So once a person is out of the body, he or she is a happy camper. However the anger and the violence that they felt as they were killed or murdered stays behind, and that's what can scare children, when they see or sense the entity.

SOLUTION

To clear away this negativity or entities, follow these instructions:

- Get a one-quart, glass Pyrex pitcher, which looks like a big measuring cup. I like that one because it's got a handle on it.

- Put in a cup of Epsom salts.

- Next add, five to seven tablespoons of Everclear (distilled spirits). Denatured alcohol works also, but Everclear is easy to get from a liquor store.

- Light the mixture with a longer fireplace lighter. Wear potholders because pitcher will get hot.

- Start at one corner of your home, on the lowest level of your house, and move upwards, walking through each room.

- Make sure you keep your face back from the pitcher, because when you hit a negative energy, the flames can rise a good foot and a half out of the mixture.

The interesting thing is the salt crystals can absorb the negative energy. That's why I use Epsom salts. The alcohol and the fire produce the medium that allows the combustion, and the flames disperse the negative energy. What's really interesting, too, when you're doing this, is that if you walk past an icon—a cross or something—the flames go out.

When the space or home is cleared, then the child who perceived the negative energy needs a healing or clearing. Emotional solutions with children include three aspects:

- They need to know they are loved.

- They need to know that they are loveable.

- They need to know they have choices, which gives them empowerment.

I think it's important also to teach children about high and low vibrations in the universe, and to always reach for that higher vibration, that better feeling. The only difference between here and there is level of vibration. The best example I can use is that when we see a hummingbird in flight, we cannot perceive its wings because the wings are beating at such a high vibration. The other side to me is exactly like that. It isn't somewhere else; it's right here. It is just that everything on the other side has such a high vibration or high frequency that we don't always see it there. We have a lower vibration because we're in these physical forms. We cannot perceive things on the other side unless we raise our own vibration.

I think the hummingbird example explains that ghosts don't come down long, dark corridors to haunt us. You know, they're right here all the time anyway. It's just a matter of what we choose to perceive.

A THREE-YEAR-OLD DEALS WITH ENTITIES

I was called to a house in Carson City, Nevada, because there was a three-year-old child who was seeing horrifying, awful things. His mom didn't see them, but the boy would stand there shaking in terror. He'd be playing, and all of a sudden, he would look up. And then he would look down and just stand there and shake. So his mom knew he wasn't making it up. He was being terrified by something that she couldn't see. I saw that he perceived not only wonderful people that were loving and kind and wanted to communicate with their loved ones, but he also saw coalesced or congealed entities of negativity that were left behind when people passed.

The mom invited me to talk to him and help, and also sense what I could in the house. They cleared the house before I got there.

When I met the child, I recognized that he was a natural medium. So he was an open channel. When you're three years old you don't understand it, nor do you have a filter, nor do you have any power to shut it off. So not only was he feeling the negative crap that was left behind from people that had passed and shed off all their negativity, but he was also seeing spirits who had passed, sitting around waiting, hoping that their loved ones were going to be in touch with him somehow.

I told him that these entities could not hurt him. Second, his mom agreed to regularly clear the house, in case her son couldn't close his channel. Finally, I taught him how to do that, and then to tell anybody that's there, "I'm only three. I can't help you. Go away." That phrase really empowered him.

I also gave him the feeling of what the crown energy center on the top of his head was like when it was open and when it was closed. I told him that when it's open, it looks like light. I drew a picture for him. I shared that that was his connection to God, and that if he didn't want to have other people having access, he can put a filter up there and only let in God's light. With crayons we drew the light and filter, and he understood.

Finally, I taught him how to ask the angels to come and protect him. And they could surround him with their wings. I've heard that he is just fine now.

The most important point is that kids don't have to go through life being terrified. They need to be empowered.

So when children see things or say that they see things or have these night terrors, parents need not wring their hands and brush off the child as a fantasist. Parents need to be proactive and believe the child, asking questions like, "What are you seeing?" and "How can I help you?" Make the child a part of that healing process, whether it's just clearing the space, which sometimes stops the problem right then and there, or getting some healing work done on that child, so the child can release an entity or become empowered.

GETTING GROUNDED

We don't have to accept negative entities becoming attached to us. It's just important to teach kids to ground, which you do with visualization and intention. Grounding empowers them.

It centers them and pulls their energy down into their bodies. A lot of times, kids get so fearful that their energy goes out the top of their head and then they feel disconnected.

TERRI JAY'S GROUNDING INSTRUCTIONS

WHAT IS GROUNDING?

Grounding is an amazing technique done with visualization and intention. It is so powerful that you can actually feel a difference in your body when you do it. The exercise consists of visualizing roots growing out of your feet and your tailbone and seeing yourself tie those roots to the center of the earth.

WHY DO WE WANT TO GROUND?

Grounding keeps you balanced, energized, healthy, and happy. It heightens your intuition and the other spiritual senses of clairvoyance (clear seeing), clairsentience (clear feeling), and clairaudience (clear hearing). It calms us down in stressful situations, energizes us when we feel depleted, and can actually keep us healthy or help us to become healthier.

HOW DO WE DO IT?

Be comfortable and relaxed, either sitting or standing, feet flat on the floor. Relax your arms and don't cross them.

First, set your intention, making it positive in nature. Say your intention to yourself, such as "I am a grounded, optimistic person." Use whatever feels right and is appropriate to your situation, as long as it is positive for you.

Next, picture roots growing out of the soles of your feet and out of your tailbone. Imagine your roots to be sparkly and stretchy white-light roots, not at all like tree or plant roots. You want the base of the root to be as big as a fist and to widen out to dinner-plate size as it moves away from your body.

Send your roots to the center of the earth, wrap them around the core of the earth, and then bring them back up to you. When you bring them up, also bring up the healing fire of the earth's core.

As they reach your feet again, have them slowly circle and surround you, moving around your body to your waist.

Next, bring the roots' energy up to about waist high and just leave it there, shimmering around you. (If you reach out your hand, you may feel warmth and tingling where your roots are.)

Practice grounding several times a day; it takes you only seconds to do this visualization. Always do this grounding before any stressful situation, whenever you are worried, or when you need healing.

Don't worry if you get goose bumps or your stomach feels fluttery. This just means you've done it correctly.

With practice, you will be able to stay grounded longer, without effort, and everything will get easier for you.

Hillary Raimo on Dreaming and Kids

Raimo offers suggestions for how parents can encourage children to daydream for creativity as well as keep records of night dreams. Other psychics interviewed for this book have discussed the dreams they had as children, some of them prophetic in nature. Some dream experiences, like ghost encounters, frighten children until they understand what the dream means. Teaching children that dreams are okay helps to bridge and strengthen their connection with their intuitive selves.

ESTABLISH RELATIONSHIPS TO DREAMS

Our dreams are windows to our souls. They allow openings into other places, other worlds, and show us aspects of ourselves we sometimes have no other way of seeing in the conscious state. We can seek guidance and communicate with other aspects of ourselves even. Dream signs help guide us in the waking state, as well as in the dream state.

Encouraging our children to have a strong relationship with dreaming is a practical way to help them understand the world of the unseen. A simple dream journal, having your kids draw their dreams, or making conversations about dreams are all wonderful ways to encourage the development of intuition. As you make it a priority to support and help guide your children, not only will it help you, as a parent, to reconnect with your own intuition, but it also shows your children that they have nothing to fear. As we build a stronger relationship with our dreams, we begin to heal the connection with our intuition. Psychic abilities come out of a strong and healthy relationship with our intuitive side.

A Son Confesses

While working on this section, I had my own experience, as a mom, with my youngest son, Michael. One night we were driving to pick up our take-out food, and out of the blue he says he sees ghosts. Michael had never said anything before.

He looked at me sideways to see what my response was, and when he realized I was calm and curious, he continued. I asked him how long this had been happening and how they appeared to him. He explained that he sees shadow ghosts and light ghosts. The shadowy ones scare him, and he sees them mostly before he goes to sleep. Recently, like me, Michael began sleeping with an eye mask, and when he does, they do not seem to be able to "pull him" as much, as he put it.

I asked him why he hadn't told me before, and he said he didn't think I'd believe him. It goes to show, no matter how much we think our kids understand they can talk to us, for whatever reason, they may not. Considering the work I do professionally as an intuitive, it was no surprise my son was having these experiences, but it was surprising that he wasn't speaking about them. In fact, Michael never said much about experiencing anything along the lines of the paranormal or psychic worlds. So when he decided that night to discuss it with me, I was surprised, but also very pleased.

Bring in the Angels

When children have these dreams or scary night experiences, one of the ways I suggest parents help their kids is to talk about bringing angels in. Most of us grew up saying our prayers before bed. Setting the intention for a blessed and sacred space to fall asleep in creates a protective web around us in that precious state between waking and sleeping, when most ghosts are able to make contact. It also protects us in our dreaming.

Make it fun, and tell your children they can call in their favorite angel before they go to bed. This sets the intention for a protective space. Dream guides work with us in our actual dreaming state, and angels can certainly be among of those dream guides.

ENCOURAGE COMMUNICATION

Keeping the lines of communication open with your child is a priority. Letting your children know that they can talk to you about anything they experience and reassuring them they won't feel weird, or outcast because of it, will give them a sense of safety as well. So talk to your child about a dream guide, make it a fun task! Have him or her draw the guide and say a few words to the guide throughout the day, as well as before bed. Encourage a strong relationship with guides and make it fun—the keys to building a strong dreaming foundation that will carry into adulthood.

When a child experiences a nightmare and gets scared, take the time to sit with them. Let them tell you the details, because in their mind, the dream is real, and the reaction they feel is normal. Validation for a child's feelings encourages them to trust themselves. We can only have a strong relationship with our dreams if we trust them. Trust is the key to creating a strong bridge between our waking world and our dreaming world.

When we draw or write down our dreams after we have them, we'll have a longer lasting impression and stronger recall. Most children will enjoy sharing the story of their dreams with you; that sharing will be like a private bond, engaging the imagination. As we write down our dreams and make time for them, it signals to our psyches that we value them. As we value our dreams more, we are also valuing ourselves, our totality.

Have your child pick out a special notebook for their dream journal. They can decorate it if they like, and maybe even buy a special pen to go with it. Have them keep it next to their bed, and when they wake up in the morning, ask them to write down or draw anything from the night before. It also makes great breakfast table conversation.

If they do not recall the whole dream, they can write down words, feelings, or images they remember. It doesn't have to make sense. Forgive spelling and grammatical errors; this is an act to engage the right brain, where symbols and less logical ideas are born. Most important, make it fun. Follow the flow!

BRIDGING THE DREAM

Another fun task is what I call bridging the dream. When your child recalls certain objects in their dreams, have them try and find that same object in waking time. For example, let's say your child dreams of wearing a green shirt the night before. Have your child wear a green shirt the next day. This bridges the dreamtime with the waking time. Each bridge shows the child that there is no difference between what we dream at night and what we experience in waking time. Understanding that dreaming is an act of manifestation means that if we can dream it, then we really can create it. Practicing bridging the dream helps kids understand this complex idea in a fun and practical way.

DAYDREAMING TIME

Conscious daydreaming is another way to help kids establish a healthy dream life. Usually children are told to not daydream and to get their heads out of the clouds. I would like to suggest giving children the space they need to actively and consciously daydream. Engaging their imaginations like this stimulates a healthy stream of creativity and provides an outlet for their active minds to explore the endless possibilities that exist out there. Daydreaming is magical and gives us permission to explore our most secret dreams and wishes in the privacy of our own minds. Encourage your children to write dreams down in a story journal that is different from their night dreaming journal.

Have them pick out a special place where they can sit or lay down for a time to daydream. My son has chosen the hammock in our backyard. I know when he is out there, he is daydreaming, and I do not interrupt him. Pick a location together, so you know when they are doing these activities and you can respect their space.

IN CONCLUSION

Dreaming is the other half of who we are. We are dreamers who carry out what we dream about whether we are aware of it or not. We are what we think, and our thoughts create our reality around us. When we understand this, we act from a more conscious viewpoint. Responsibility for our actions becomes a side effect. When we consciously dream our lives, we empower those lives with our spirit, and we practice the art of balancing the physical, emotional, spiritual, and mental aspects of ourselves naturally.

Our children are the hope for our future and the keepers of our planet. If they can dream a new way of being and trust that it can manifest, then true change is possible.

Melissa Peil's Meetup Support Group

*What usually has the strongest psychic effect on the child
is the life that the parents have not lived.*

—CARL JUNG

Can there ever be enough mentoring and positive support for families whose kids see ghosts and have connections to the other side? Melissa Peil *(www.mysticalawakenings.com)* is a psychic, medium, and teacher who has a passion for helping people, and she and I agree that this is one group of children who need advocacy. Because Peil is an expert on advocacy for intuitive children, I've asked her to contribute her thoughts on supporting parents and children who see ghosts. She has organized and facilitated a Meetup group for intuitive children and their families.

Peil's professional experience includes teaching elementary school. She is now pursuing her dream of working with intuitive children, helping them understand and embrace their gifts while working with their families to provide the best possible environment.

ADVOCACY FOR KIDS WHO SEE GHOSTS

Being in touch with our spiritual side can be quite difficult for some adults. This is not the case, however, for children. Most children are free from activities like careers and relationships, which engulf adults. Without having any kind of filters on their outlook on life, most children are able to be in touch with their spiritual side. As humans continue to evolve, the sensitivity of children increases, and they are more in touch with the other side.

Growing up as an intuitive child had its challenges. I was sensitive to others' feelings. I knew things would happen before they did. Being a psychic, medium, and teacher, I have worked with many children who are sensitive to their environments and have intuitive abilities. Their spiritual gifts come in many forms: the power to heal others around them, empathic abilities to feel others emotions, and seeing ghosts or other spirit people.

In my own experience, seeing ghosts was not so scary because I was born with intuitive talents. However, I knew that I was different from the other kids, and other children who have these precious gifts around the globe experience similar feelings of isolation.

A child's world can be lonely and confusing when you know you are different from your peers. It is also sad when a child is struggling to discover who they are in this big world—finding their niche and seeing where they fit in—yet doesn't feel comfortable being truly themselves. Such situations are eased when an adult in a child's social network supports him or her.

Some children muster up what courage they can to tell someone about their paranormal experiences. When a trustworthy parent or adult turns on them, this breaks the trust that the child thought existed in their relationships. It alienates the child even more than they already were, and from here, the downward spiral begins for children with special gifts.

In a downward spiral, you'll notice a child withdraw from regular activities that were once enjoyable. For example, one second-grade student, who saw ghosts and was connected to the spirit realm, closed off to friendships he admired, withdrew from his family by staying in his room for hours on end, staring at the wall, and eventually stopped speaking to anyone. His school-work plummeted, and he lost all motivation to work. This boy's spirit was crushed; he was now an outsider. He felt as if he had nowhere to turn and lacked any tools to return to a circle that was once happy and safe. This example is a prime reason we need to support and connect with our children and meet their needs.

WHY A MEETUP HELPS

Why would a Meetup for parents and kids who see ghosts be helpful? What are the benefits? I had the opportunity to work with multiple families of indigo children. In the fall of 2007, I created a support group, Families of Indigo Children, through *www.meetup.com*. This website is geared toward anyone looking to connect with others with common interests. Meetups are free for members to join, though there is a fee for the organizer to maintain the group through the website.

Families of Indigo Children welcomed parents and children to come together and share their experiences. This was important to me because I saw the detrimental effects that children experienced as a result of seeing spirits. Families had no place to turn. These children felt alienated, weird, and were socially outcast within their peer groups.

A benefit of this Meetup group was that it provided an outlet for the children and their families. All came together and developed a sense of belonging, which was lacking in their daily lives. Children who came to this group with their parents were shy at first. When their parents told them that it was safe to speak about their experiences, relationships formed among the children. Once this happened, the parents connected with one another.

Before long, conversations were happening among different families. They discussed how they coped with the pressures put on them by school officials who are bound and determined to find something wrong with their child. They shared how their children experienced difficulties eating because of sensitivities to different textures of food.

The Families of Indigo Children Meetup connected people who would otherwise never have met one another because of the shameful feeling that comes along with the fact their children "see dead people." The group provided a sense of security, trust, and compassion for children who are spiritually in tune. The members of this group felt a sense of belonging and formed their own community—something that had been nonexistent for a while.

FACILITATING THE MEETUP

I was there as a facilitator who wanted to see bonds made between families and children who were struggling with the same issues. My background as a teacher as well as a psychic-medium (who sees spirits) made me a resource and allowed me to also offer group classes to help them move through fears of the unknown.

As a teacher, I was aware of the importance of belonging to a group of peers. Group classes gave the kids a chance to express themselves and also to learn from one another. Children felt supported in this class-type environment not only because they had peers to relate to but also because I was their mentor. It is important for children to have someone they can trust who can relate to them. I have an advantage as their spiritual mentor that many of their parents do not—I have the spiritual gift of being psychic and a medium, and to see spirits just as they do. I have been able to show them that even though going through life with these gifts can be scary and uncertain, there is a light at the end of the tunnel and that good things can come from having these gifts. I show this to them leading by example. I allow them the openness to make mistakes, talk about their feelings (particularly fear), and I curb their fear by enriching their lives with knowledge.

More important, the kids I work with know how much I care. As a wise educator once said, "Kids don't care how much you know until they know how much you care." How true this is.

The class for parents would be structured in the same manner, of talking about what happened with their kids that week we could celebrate and about what some stuggles were. I would be able to help them come up with strategies based on my experience as a teacher, Other parents in the group also contributed to the conversation by offering what worked for them in difficult situations. At the end, I would provide them with the next topic to be covered in class, provide websites where parents could find further topic information. Then, if their child talked about a class topic, the parents would be able to have a meaningful conversation with their child. Ideally, topics would be laid out for the month well in advance so that parents could research the topics at their leisure and possibly carry on conversations with their child(ren) ahead of time. The classes provided a wonderful resource for parents and children alike.

Parents benefited through a connection with one another—they were able to talk about their challenges raising intuitive children—but that connection would also educate them on what their children truly experience (such as seeing auras around people, seeing spirits, or the intuitive knowing about things before they happen). As you can imagine, this is a full commitment for the parents and children involved, but a necessary one for many families. The Meetup opened a door for parents to talk about their children with someone who would understand in a way that a psychologist or school counselor would not.

A true leader for a Meetup group like this must approach it with heart. Otherwise the leader's intention may be misinterpreted as trying to gather new clients for their business. Many groups fail for that exact reason. Staying strong, with a vision in mind, and putting that vision out there allowed our group to thrive because there were no hidden agendas.

GROUP MEMBERSHIP EXPANDS

Our group chose to meet once per month. In retrospect, it would have been more beneficial for members to have two meetings offered within the month on different days of the week so that members would have more chances to participate and connect with others.

Meetup groups typically meet in public settings at first, and after the members get to know one another and establish a community, some groups move their meetings to members' homes. This was the case with the Families of Indigo Children group. We originally met in a local coffee shop. The first event was for parents to meet with one another; to meet me, the organizer; and to get a feel for where this group was headed. After our group's initial meeting, we convened at one member's home consistently.

Opening up one's home to the group was an excellent idea for many reasons. Children came with their parents and took part in our circle, discussing the gifts they had and the struggles they encountered. Because we were in a private residence, there was a sense of trust and safety. The fear of being overheard in public by someone who has a different outlook on the topic was gone. Instead, a sense of love and acceptance was immanent. Younger children were welcome to play together outside in the yard with an adult who stayed there to supervise. The setup of using a person's home for a group like this was exactly what our members needed. As the organizer, I saw this as an opportunity to take connecting the group members to another level.

Before long, this group not only had families of indigo children, but also members from our area who wanted to help. Jenna Forrest, an author specializing in sensitive children, joined and was invited to present what she knew to our group. One of our members had been a Montessori teacher for years, and another member/parent had a great deal of experience working with nonverbal autistic children. Another member was an astrologist who helped families gain understanding of their children based on what was in the stars for them. We became a dynamic group who helped these intuitive children and their families.

In Conclusion

Approaching my community with an open mind and compassionate heart best served this community because it gave them someone to talk to who had their best interests in mind. Families needed a forum in which to connect with others and to ask questions they felt silly asking professionals (particularly when it came to validating whether or not their children were seeing spirits), so they could see they were not alone on this journey of raising intuitive or indigo children.

In conclusion, Meetup groups are a fabulous way to connect with and find support from others in your local area. Without having the support you desire, you can feel extremely alienated and like you don't belong. A Meetup group offers a way to explore and to meet your needs and your child's needs. I highly recommend that you seek out these resources within your community.

GUIDELINES FOR FACILITATING YOUR MEETUP GROUPS OR CLASSES

Purpose:
- Provide a sense of comfort and community.
- Welcome parents and children together at a home.

Introduction:
- Facilitator shares and discusses the specific gifts each child has.
- Facilitator gauges what needs exist for the parents.
- Facilitator determines the needs of the children.
- Facilitator monitors the level of knowledge that parents and children have in certain subject areas for planning topics for classes or meetings.

Children's Classes:
- Talk about the children's week and how it's gone.
- Discuss any weird happenings, such as seeing ghosts, or whatever they feel the need to share. (Sharing is facilitated so every child has an opportunity to talk if they desire.)
- Introduce a topic of the day to expand concepts.
- Introduce a hands-on learning activity.

The benefits of introducing new topics: Sometimes, a kid might know a topic or be able to identify with it, but never had the words for it. One example in Peil's group was a child who saw auras. When auras were described as colors around someone, he said "I see that all the time!" and it sparked immediate interest for him. His mom was just as surprised as anyone because he'd never told her he saw colors around people!

The benefits of learning activities: Providing a hands-on learning activity makes the learning more meaningful for the students. It is always such a satisfying feeling to be able to see the smile on a child's face when they are in their element of success! Taking it to the next level is when children who appear sad, depressed, withdrawn, and introverted become happy, smiling, and engaged. For these kids, knowing they are supported in areas that are their strengths feeds their self-images. They are in a loving environment where anything goes, and their true self can shine.

Parent participation: Once the children's Meetup group or class is set up, the facilitator should consult with the parents individually before bringing them into the children's class. Parents are always welcome to accompany their child to the group, see the different children's talents, and stay long enough for their child to feel comfortable to be on his or her own.

Parents' Classes:
- Talk about parental challenges.
- Provide the opportunity for other parents to answer questions.
- Discuss such experiences as seeing spirits or ghosts. Share beliefs and feelings about such sightings.
- Teach them about the things their children go through.

Susan Gale on the Heart and Nature

The transformational teachings that intuitive teacher Susan Gale offers through A Place of Light in Massachusetts focus on the Native American philosophy of connection to nature and also to the heart within the self.

The success of the recommendations Gale makes here is well documented in her work and demonstrated in the stories she shares. She says:

- Do not push frightened, scared children in a direction that doesn't suit their nature.

- The easiest and most loving way to honor a child's nature is to give them choices.

- To calm a child's fears or to help them manage stress, it is beneficial for them to go outside, return to nature, and connect with it again.

- Teach children to return to their heart during those times when they can't go outside.

EVERYONE HAS THE ABILITY TO SEE GHOSTS

When you walk in the woods and see a beautiful animal, the first thing you feel is from your heart because it's that energy connection. The animals live in their heart. They don't dwell in their mind. So the first thing you feel is being connected with all things.

To me, it's very natural to walk in the woods, be free, and live off the land, and I teach children that. I teach them how to track, listen, feel, and sense things when they sit still. You can put your energy way out there, and you can feel when something is moving. The children can recognize the feeling and name what it is. A squirrel, a chipmunk, a turkey, a rabbit—they will know what it is before they've seen it. Society will teach that is not possible. You have to see it with your eyes to be able to identify it, right? Well, not true!

When we came into this world, our spirits were still fresh. Our shell is a new shell that we have. So everything is a beautiful learning process. As we get older, society teaches us to stray from that, like there's no such thing as spirits. Yet there are religions that believe in these spirits that are no longer on this earth, right?

To me, it's just a matter of figuring out how you want to walk—in your heart. Or do you want to walk in your mind? People who tend to walk in their hearts grow and prosper. They help many. They do great things, and being around them is just beautiful.

THE HEART AFFECTS CHANGE

For example, one of the children who attended A Place of Light was getting to the age of going to school, and his parents didn't let him do pre-kindergarten because they [the pre-kindergarten teachers and students] would not have understood him. He used to play with his great-grandmother and other spirit people that had passed. (Well, their shells had passed, but their spirits hadn't.) He would play with them all the time. People wouldn't understand that.

He was able to walk up and hug a person and change their mood. If they were sad and crying, he could change their mood. He could hold them and put that love and energy into them, and then they were happy.

When the boy went into kindergarten, his father explained to the teacher, "Look, we believe the traditional way—the way the Native Americans always have. We believe in spirits, we believe in many things that most people don't. So if he's doing something that's a little odd to you, look at it and observe it first before you judge it. Then if there's a problem, give me a call, and I'll come in and explain it." The teacher agreed to do so.

In the first couple of weeks of school, all the young children that get dropped off start crying. Well, the son walked up to them and started hugging them and giving them love. Two minutes later the children were running around, playing, and they forgot the separation anxiety. The teacher watched him do this throughout the day with different children. If they were arguing and fighting, he would go up and shift their energy.

One day she came in, and she was not feeling good. She was grumpy. She had had a bad morning and arrived late. The boy walked up to her and said, "You need some love." He gave her a hug and shifted her energy. It made her nervous and excited, but she didn't know what to do. So she excused herself from the room and called his father, telling him, "I need you to come as soon as you can."

He got the visitor's pass at the school office and went to her class and asked, "What's the problem?" She says, "Oh no, there's no problem. I just had to give you a hug and thank you for explaining things to me. I don't know how he does it, but it's amazing and beautiful."

She asked if the father could help her learn, so he showed her how to shift the energy in her children where they could be more comfortable, and they didn't have to cry when their parents left.

Just Change Their Energy Through Nature

Instead of trying to talk to them and make them feel better that way, just to change their energy.

—Susan Gale

When you're talking to people, you're talking to the mind. It's the heart that you want to work with, and sometimes there are no words for what needs to be done. Everybody has his or her own way. To me, I just share the love of all the beautiful things that I've seen and felt within my lifetime, and I embrace the person with that.

The most beautiful thing I love to do is bring people to the woods next to a river, water, animals, trees, a lot of greenery. Once they feel that energy, they shift quickly. If you take somebody away from the city and go out into nature together, they feel the vibration, and they love it. We share together. People forget where their true roots come from. We all come from Mother Earth, and we are all part of her. So Mother Earth provides for us. She gives us everything, and in return we're supposed to respect her. It's a balance.

People will keep that memory for the rest of their lives. And they can use that memory whenever they're in a bad spot.

I ran a children's camp for twelve years, and we always took the children out in the woods every morning. One girl, a counselor in training, went out for an hour by herself. One hour is a long time for a city child. Afterwards, she said, "I never knew how beautiful it could be." She was fourteen at the time. Then she lost her way, and I didn't see her for several years.

When she was around eighteen, all of a sudden, we linked up. I returned with her to the beautiful lake, her memory of Mother Earth. She drew it all inside her like a final deep breath. Then she died the next day. I think she knew that the path she had taken was going to lead her to that early death, but she went back to nature's beauty to sustain her soul. Returning all children to nature is huge. To be comfortable in the woods, to be comfortable around animals, to appreciate the creepy crawlers—to appreciate all of that by the time they're four or five years old insures that it will never leave them.

STRATEGIES FOR WORKING WITH SPIRITS

One of the biggest reasons kids see spirit walkers is because children haven't forgotten how to use their abilities; spirits tend to linger near kids who can see them, feel them, or hear them. In many cases, spirit people want to be heard, to say something, or even to make friendships in a lot of ways.

We in the flesh forget about the spirit part. Today's movies portray most of these spirits as bad and evil, and that's not true. You can find good in anything if you really look. No matter how bad it is or how bad the person is, you can find good in it. If you find that good, that's where you can grow and learn.

I've had children come to me who say, "I have spirits bothering me all the time, even when I'm at school. I can't concentrate. I hear voices. I hear sounds." I tell them to pick a certain time to deal with the spirits. So every day, between 6 and 7 p.m., tell them, "I will speak with you then. I will help you, but it has to be one at a time, and when the hours are done, that's it. I need my personal time. I need to go play. I need to go read a book. I need to study for school. I need to do things, too." Spirits listen. They're just like us; they just don't have a concept of time.

Go ahead and make your choices. Take control of your life and your time. When I help people from the spirit world, I pick and choose my time. I don't want them bothering me when I'm taking a shower. I don't want them bothering me when I'm trying to eat or work with a client.

The only time I'll allow spirits to come in and interfere is when the client wants to speak to that spirit or when that spirit has something important to talk to that client about. I'll describe the spirit to the client and give them as much information as possible, and then I'll ask the client if they want to connect. If not, then I'll send the spirit away. If so, then we will let it speak. Ninety-five percent of the time they'll let the spirit speak, and then the spirit will never bother them again. The message just had to come through.

Here are some pointers for children who see and connect with spirit walkers:

- There's always a place to get what you need. Don't ever feel that you're abandoned.

- If you do feel alone, ask the Creator, or whomever you believe in, to give you the energy of love to shift things around you— to open your parents' ears and eyes, so they would be more willing to learn also. Ask your parents if they've ever heard or seen or felt psychic. Ask your aunt, uncle, or grandmother. Someone in the family will remember, because this ability does run in families.

The only limitations there are the ones we put in front of us. If a druggie's energy from the next apartment is so negative and pushing your way, push it back and say, "I don't want any part of it. Just keep it. That's yours. I'll send you some love also and maybe that will help you change your way."

If the energy or ghosts in a certain room frighten you, then change the energy in the room. Take control. Go in there, sit there, and change the energy. Paint rainbows in the air. Think of a very beautiful place and then push that energy out and all around the room. Then say, "I'm leaving this energy here." If you leave it there, nothing negative will go there. By taking control of your environment, you can be true to yourself and stay safe.

One thing that helps people understand the fear is what I call it an E.T. moment. In the movie *E.T.*, when the little sister met E.T., she screamed, E.T. screamed, and then everybody screamed. When you act like that little girl, you frighten the spirit people as much as you feel frightened by them.

Expect the same of spirit people that you would expect of people with physical bodies. You would expect good manners. You wouldn't let people come into your room at will if they were physical people. You wouldn't expect to look up and see twenty people in your bathroom. Make your choices and take control of your environment.

Here are other strategies that work for children:

• Imagine a radio with a dial, and when the sound is too much, just turn the volume down.

• When spirit people need to go to the light or another place, create a staircase wherever you are, and when spirits come around, you can say, "There's the way to the light. There are people on the other side whose job is to help people cross over. Watch for helpers at the top of the staircase." Then let them go up.

I was in Texas once, and my geographic location had such a heavy feeling. So one morning I went out very early and put up staircases, like, every fifty feet, and I could see whole families holding hands and running up. I found out later that the location had been a sugarcane plantation. You can imagine the agony people went through that had to work those fields. The place felt lighter afterwards, and other people noticed how much better it felt. I know of many who have made the staircases and just left them permanently.

When you're walking in love and when you're projecting love, it's like two notes on the piano. Love doesn't harmonize with negativity, and so negativity can't be around you so much. If negativity is around you, then you aren't comfortable, because there's no harmony for it.

If you're afraid, if you're hurt, or if you're depressed, then the negativity will harmonize with you, and you keep it around. Some people have to work hard to keep themselves in that positive place where they won't harmonize with negative things. For example, empathic children, who feel others' energy, need to learn to push out their energy and not allow negative things to come to them. Those are some of the things we do to learn how to take it when somebody is pushing bad energy on you and how to keep it off you. These are techniques that you can learn and use.

Donna Seebo on Children Learning to Trust Intuition

Seebo explains how natural seeing ghosts is for children—as natural as smelling fragrant flowers—because children's perception of reality is so different from adults' viewpoints. Also Seebo tells the story of a teen who saw a frightening ghost who was trying to communicate with her. Through Seebo's mentoring, the young woman came to understand why the ghost contacted her and what she learned from the frightening experience.

When people are in a particular level of receptivity, they are sensitive to various spiritual or psychic experiences. What you want a child to know and understand is these experiences are as natural as breathing and not to be feared. How many times have we watched horror flicks where ghosts terrified people, creating great harm and discord? This is not what you want to convey into a young child's mind.

Young children do not know reality as adults do. The physical world as we know it is not separate from the alternate reality or the other side. A child's reality is what they are going through in any given moment, without time boundaries. Some children will have spirit friends that can be people or animals. They may see various energy forms that could be described as fairies. Children are seeing a vibratory frequency that adults have taught themselves not to see. Should they share their stories of their friends with you, be wise and listen thoughtfully, perhaps even encouraging them to draw what they see for you. You might be quite surprised at what they share.

TALKING TO FLOWERS

Have you ever noticed a child talking to plants, flowers, or trees? I have. Luther Burbank was a renowned botanist, horticulturist, and pioneer in the science of agriculture in the late 1800s and early 1900s. From his earliest recall, he talked to plants. Fortunately for him, his parents did not make fun of this behavior. He said that plants responded to his conversations and would share their secrets with him. Through this unique communication, he learned to patiently observe and listen. The plants taught him how to use them to make some of the changes he wanted to make, improving their structure on many levels. What empowered Burbank was this innate understanding and respect for plant life. As a consequence, he developed better potatoes that withstood blight and made many other changes that brought betterment to the world of food development.

Burbank was a good friend of Paramahansa Yogananda, who taught his followers in America and India the need for direct experiences and called intuition the doorway to knowing God. They would often discuss Burbank's experiences of communication with various life-forms. Burbank believed that to truly understand nature, you must honor and respect all life in all of its forms.

Albert Schweitzer was of the same mind-set. He often wrestled with himself, as he was a physician and he did not believe in killing any form of life; yet as a physician, when he was dealing with horrific diseases out in the middle of Africa, he would say, "Every time I use an antiseptic I am killing life." He had this empathy, a deep respect and appreciation, for life, and it became stronger as he got older.

A GHOST APPEARS TO EXPLAIN HIS DEATH

I've worked with children and adults who see spirits all the time. One client I remember was brought to me by her mother, who was both upset and intrigued with what her daughter was going through.

The daughter, whom I'll call Lynn, shared that a family member had died a violent death that was traumatic to the entire family, especially her mother. This relative had been involved in narcotics and was coming back and visiting Lynn, who didn't know what to do with these visits. Nothing like this had ever happened to her before.

I asked her why she was afraid, and she told me this male relative would materialize in her presence, wanting her to recognize him. He was trying to communicate that there were extenuating circumstances with his death. He showed himself exactly as he was after the accident when he died. She had not seen any photos or been told about what the accident's conditions were like.

The communications were increasing in intensity and were occurring more frequently, and Lynn was becoming frightened by them. The only person she could talk to was her mother, and the stories were scaring her badly, as she didn't understand what was going on. She couldn't speak at all to the other family members regarding these incidences.

I said to this young woman, "Everyone is different. This may be the only experience like this you will have in your lifetime, but you need to respect it and appreciate it. This person, for whatever reason, is able to communicate with you. There is a capacity of communication with you that he isn't able to make with anyone else. He hasn't visited anyone else in the family. He is trying to tell you what happened, and I think he wants to let you know he is okay."

Lynn didn't understand why the relative was first showing himself as he looked after the horrific accident and then as happy and fine. I explained that he's conveying a few things: He's alive in the sense that he's on the other side. He wanted Lynn to know about certain points of information on the accident and to clear up confusion. Finally, he seemed to communicate to Lynn that he's sorry for the stupid things that he did that caused this situation to evolve. By the time Lynn and I were finished, she was relaxed and felt comfortable about her psychic situation.

Anyone who has these psychic episodes should ask themselves, "Why am I in this space? What am I to learn? Is there action I need to take? Is there information I need to have or know?"

INCREASING PSYCHIC CAPACITIES

Today I am seeing and talking with lots of people who are experiencing an intensity of intuitive perceptiveness. This is occurring with all age groups. It's quite amazing, to say the least.

We're experiencing an increase in intuitive perception be-cause it is necessary for the survival of the species. There is this heightened awareness in the current era, and we are going to have choices. We're either going to prepare ourselves so that we are able to move forward rapidly, regardless of our age, or we are going to be in the dark ages. Our proactive sensory awareness is evolving with purpose.

When it comes to kids who see ghosts, the important points are clarity and making them aware that they will feel different feelings, such as the sensation of heat or coldness affecting their physical body and surroundings. There may be heightened sen-sations with smells or sounds. They may hear conversations that no one else in the room can hear.

All of these things should be paid attention to and not exag-gerated. At these moments, a wise parent will have a book or material available on famous mediums like Arthur Ford, Irene Garret, Edgar Cayce, or other well-known mediums.

DON'T UNDERESTIMATE THE KIDS

I would like to tell parents to not underestimate children. People ask me how seeing energies like ghosts or spirits contributes to children's lives in a positive way. One, the children will realize that life goes on and cannot be destroyed. Two, they are not ever alone. And three, they may be given communication to share with others that will make a difference in someone's life.

When your child has this capacity of phenomenal imagina-tion, you don't want to encourage exaggeration, but do encour-age curiosity and discovery. On the next page are some things you may want to bring up for clarity and information about what they perceive.

- "Show me what it is you say. Or better yet, draw it for me."

- "Show me how you feel what you are sensing."

- "If you didn't see a form, then what colors do you see?" Let the child use crayons to draw what they perceive. Don't comment while they are doing it; just observe.

- "Can you tell me what it looks like?" If they're experiencing an alternate dimension, it may have color tones or texture that, if you're not careful, may cause you to interpret it as something very bad. Don't judge. Instead, observe and listen carefully.

- "Did it move? How big is it? Is it thick? Hot? Cold? Wide? Narrow?" Use your hands to help describe what they tell you.

- Perhaps you may want to step outside. If a child has had an astral-projection experience, they may have experienced a sense of flying. Did they have a feeling of space as big as the sky?

In summary, we ask children to define their awareness in as concrete terms and description as possible—tactile, kinesthetic, auditory, etc. Don't be afraid to inquire, don't be afraid of psychic experiences, and don't elaborate or exaggerate the child's perception. It is what it is!

Conclusion

We took the subject of kids who see ghosts out of the darkness of superstition and fear and brought it into the light. Through the eyes, words, and feelings of other parents and professionals, you've walked the rim of the circle and viewed the subject from different angles. You now:

- know that neuroscience in the last decade has enabled our understanding of children's neural development, brain-wave states, and learning paths.

- know that there are more children seeing ghosts than ever before, and the trend is expected to continue.

- understand that the ability to see spirits seems to run in families.

- have learned that children can have one isolated episode or can have an intuitive talent that is part of their character.

- know that kids develop a specific worldview in which seeing spirit walkers may or may not be included.

- understand that fear is a healthy response and helps children learn discernment and helps children transform fear into empowered actions.

- know that it is all right to observe your child's behavior in relation to seeing ghosts before taking him or her to a medical specialist. Take notes, use logic, and be clear in reporting specific behaviors to your health-care practitioner.

- know to use common sense when approaching situations in which kids see ghosts, to not dramatize, and to be honest in your feelings as an adult.

- understand that you should listen to your children and then listen some more. Ask questions and keep an open mind. Every person interviewed stated this advice in different ways.

- realize that empowerment means helping your child develop confidence and the ability to take action and be proactive in his or her environment.

- know to treat spirit walkers like regular folks by having discussions with them, asking them questions, defining boundaries when interacting with them, telling them to go away, or being of service to them.

- know that art, music, play, and other expressive outlets are helpful for creative children who see ghosts.

- know that getting centered and grounded in nature also helps children who see ghosts.

- know that martial arts, like karate, teach children character and empowerment through movement.

- know that dream journaling and storytelling can be used to engage your child's creativity and openness.

- know that once a child or adult has contact with the alternate reality or other side, such as through near-death experiences or seeing ghosts, the doorway seems to stay open. The person appears connected unless he or she makes a definite choice to close that door.

- understand that you don't have to believe in spirits to help children feel empowered and be able to deal with what they see. An open heart and ear are all that's required.

Kids who see ghosts may be sensitive, have strong intuitive intelligence, or be intuitive learners. You can read more about the five types of intuitive intelligences in *Raising Intuitive Children* (New Page, 2009) by Caron B. Goode and Tara Paterson.

On the other hand, kids who see ghosts may have had a stressed-out day, and after one or two crisis apparitions, their experiences are over. It is up to the parent or primary caregiver to determine how best to assist and empower their children and themselves at the same time.

Interviewee Bios

A special thanks to the following people, who graciously allowed me to interview them for this book:

Andye Murphy and **Gavin Harrill:** Andye is a medium and intuitive counselor (*www.AndyeMurphy.com*) and her partner Gavin is an empathic psychotherapist. They are parents and the cofounders of Psychic Kids & Teens Support Group (*www.PeeKSgroup.com*), where they provide a support system for intuitive children and teens to feel valued and understood.

Athena A. Drewes, Psy.D. RPT-S, is a licensed child psychologist, parapsychologist, and consultant to the Rhine Research Center and the Parapsychology Foundation on children's psychic experiences. She has conducted research, written articles and reviews, and spoken on children and ESP, as well as had her own psychic experiences as a child through adulthood. She is a specialist in Play Therapy and is the author of *Blending Play Therapy with Cognitive Behavioral Therapy: Evidence-Based and Other Effective Treatments and Techniques* (2009) and co-author of *Cultural Issues in Play Therapy* (2006).

Brad Steiger (*www.bradandsherry.com*) started as a paranormal researcher and has evolved into a renowned author of over 170 books of miracle stories, ghost hauntings, and other paranormal topics. He is a frequent guest on radio and television and is a humorous, motivating speaker.

Donna Seebo is the author of *Mind's Magic* and host of the radio talk show the Donna Seebo Show (*www.delphiinternational.com*). She is an internationally acclaimed psychic counselor and mentalist.

Doreen Fisher, founder and CEO of Rainbow Outsourcing (*www.rainbowoutsourcing.com*) in Plano, Texas, is also the mom of two intuitive children who see ghosts. She is the consummate musician who fills her heart and her home.

Hillary Raimo (*www.hillaryraimo.com*) left a lucrative career in real estate to pursue her next career as an intuitive healer and paranormal researcher. Hillary is the author of *Money Matters: Understanding Your Relationship with Abundance* (2007) and contributes regularly to holistic health magazines. She is also a talk show host on worldwide Internet radio.

Joe Nickell, Ph.D. is "the modern Sherlock Homes," employed as the only full-time professional paranormal investigator (*www.joenickell.com*). Over the last forty years he has investigated historical documents, relics, and paranormal events and has authored 25 books on the topics of his investigations.

John Holland (*www.johnholland.com*) is an internationally renowned medium and spiritual teacher and a well-known author. He has been lecturing, teaching, demonstrating, and reading for private clients for over seventeen years. He hosts his own radio show called *Spiritual*

Connections. Holland's most recent book is *The Spirit Whisperer*: *Chronicles of a Medium.*

Kathleen Dunham, author, parent, and professional shares the ghost story from her childhood.

Lynn Andrews (*www.lynnandrews.com*) is respected teacher of shamanic principles as explained and taught in her bestselling books. She is a facilitator of consciousness through classes and workshops.

Melissa Peil (*www.mysticalawakenings.com*) started her career as a second grade teacher and, like others before her, felt called to follow the path of her natural intuition after the passing of her grandfather. She is a medium and offers clarity and insight through readings and teaching.

Michael Mendizza is an author, educator, documentary filmmaker, and founder of Touch the Future, a nonprofit learning design center (*www.ttfuture.org*). His book, *Magical Parent, Magical Child: The Art of Joyful Parenting*, co-authored with Joseph Chilton Pearce, applies research on optimum states to parenting and education.

P. M. H. Atwater (*pmhatwater.blogspot.com*) is a prolific author of eight books and an international authority and researcher on near-death states. As a survivor of several near-death experiences, her support and research have helped thousands of people understand what happened to them. She has served two terms on the Board of the International Association for Near-Death Studies and received numerous awards.

Robert Flower, Ph.D. is the founder of the Gilchrist Institute (*www.gilchristinstitute.com*), which supports Achievement Sciences, a novel scientific yet humanist approach to creating, organizing, and functioning on all levels of understanding and advancing thinking skills. His discovery of Natural Intelligence and Thinking and the New Natural Laws have been the topic of his three books and provide the basis for his consulting practice.

Sensei Robert Tallack has studied martial arts all his life. He was born into a family of martial arts professionals. Robert's mother, Sharon Berman, is a 4th Degree Black Belt, and his father, Kyoshi Ken Tallack is an 8th Degree Black Belt. Robert's goal is to spread the benefits of martial arts and character development to children across Canada through the expansion of his Karate Kids Canada Programs (*www.karatekids.ca*).

Sonia Choquette (*www.soniachoquette.com*), parent and author of several books, including the New York Times bestseller *The Answer Is Simple....*
Love Yourself, Live Your Spirit, is an internationally acclaimed intuitive guide and teacher.

Susan Gale, a parent and intuitive teacher, is the author of *Soulful Parenting*. Gale offers transformational teachings to parents and intuitive children at A Place of Light in Massachusetts.

Terri Jay (*www.terrijay.com*) is a psychic medium and energy healer offering readings and private sessions. Jay is the author of *Intuitive Messenger Bootcamp Manual*

Resources

Andrews, Lynn. *Crystal Woman*. New York: Tarcher Press, 2002.

———. *Jaguar Woman*. New York: Tarcher Press, 2007.

———. *Medicine Woman*. New York: Tarcher Press, 2006.

———. *Spirit Woman*. New York: Tarcher Press, 2007.

Atwater, P. M. H. *Beyond the Light: What Isn't Being Said About Near Death Experience . . . from Visions of Heaven to Glimpses of Hell*. Kill Devil Hills, NC: Transpersonal Publishing, 2009.

———. *The Big Book of Near Death Experiences: The Ultimate Guide to What Happens When We Die*. San Francisco: Hampton Roads Publishers, 2007.

Choquette, Sonia. *The Intuitive Spark: Brining Intuition Home to Your Child, Your family and You*. Carlsbad, CA: Hay House, 2007.

———. *Soul Lessons and Soul Purpose: A Channeled Guide to Why You Are Here*. Carlsbad, CA: Hay House, 2007.

Drewes, Athena A. "Dr. Louisa Rhine's letters revisited: The children." *Journal of Parapsychology* (vol. 66), 2002.

Drewes, Athena A., and Sally A. Drucker. *Parapsychological Research with Children: An Annotated Bibliography*. Metuchen, NJ: The Scarecrow Press, 1991.

———. *School-Based Play Therapy.* Hoboken, NJ: Wiley Publications, 2010.

Feather, Sally Rhine, and Michael Schmicker. *The Gift: ESP, the Extraordinary Experiences of Ordinary People.* New York: St. Martin's Press, 2005.

Flower, Robert. *Decoding Potential: Pathways to Understanding.* Bronxville, NY: Gilchrist Institute, 2006.

———. *A Revolution in Understanding.* Bronxville, New York: Gilchrist Institute, 2007.

———. *Your Exceptional Mind.* Bronxville, New York: Gilchrist Institute, 2008.

Gale, Susan, and Peggy Day. *Soulful Parenting: How to Embrace, Engage, and Encourage Our Children.* Virginia Beach, VA: A. R. E. Press, 2008.

Goode, Caron. *Nurture Your Child's Gift, Inspired Parenting.* Hillsboro, OR: Beyond Words, 2001.

———. *The Art & Science of Coaching Parents.* Fort Worth, TX: Inspired Living International, 2007.

Goode, Caron, and Tara Paterson. *Raising Intuitive Children: Guide Children to Know and Trust Their Gifts.* Franklin Lakes, NJ: New Page Books, 2009.

Goode, Caron, Tom Goode, and David Russell. *Help Kids Cope with Stress & Trauma.* Fort Worth, TX: Inspired Living International, 2006.

Holland, John. *Born Knowing: A Medium's Journey—Accepting and Embracing My Spiritual Gifts.* Carlsbad, CA: Hay House, 2003.

———. *Psychic Navigator.* Carlsbad, CA: Hay House, 2003.

Mathews, Ryan, and Watts Wacker. *The Deviant's Advantage.* New York: Crown Business, 2002.

Mendizza, Michael, and Joseph Chilton Pearce. *Magical Parent, Magical Child.* Berkeley, CA: North Atlantic Books, 2004.

Nickell, Joe. *Adventures in Paranormal Investigation*. Lexington, KY: The University Press of Kentucky, 2007.

——— . *Real or Fake: Studies in Authentication*. Lexington, KY: The University Press of Kentucky, 2009.

Northrup, Christiane. *Women's Bodies, Women's Wisdom*. London: Bantam, 2002.

Raimo, Hillary. *Money Matters: Understanding Your Relationship with Abundance*. Bloomington, IN: AuthorHouse, 2009.

Steiger, Brad. *Beyond Shadow World*. San Antonio, TX: Anomalist Books, 2007.

——— . *ESP: Your Sixth Sense*. Nottinghamshire: Award Books, 1967.

——— .*Real Ghosts, Restless Spirits, and Haunted Places*. Canton, MI: Visible Ink Press, 2003.

——— . *Shadow World*. San Antonio, TX: Anomalist Books, 2007.

——— . *Worlds Before Our Own*. San Antonio, TX: Anomalist Books, 2007.

Taleb, Nassim Nicholas. *The Black Swan*. New York: Random House, 2007.

Tanous, Alex, and Katherine Fair Donnelly. *Is Your Child Psychic?* New York: Macmillan, 1979.

Young, Samuel H. *Psychic Children*. Garden City, NY: Doubleday, 1977.

About *the* Author

Caron Goode is an inspirational speaker, psychotherapist, and spiritual coach. Gifted with compassion and a deep desire to assist others in expressing their passion and potential, Goode is a well-respected leader in the parent coaching industry as the founder of the Academy for Coaching Parents International that trains students in Heartwise™ coaching and parenting. Appearing in over 300 publications, including *Fort Worth Child, Woman's World, Parents Magazine, Mothering,* and *Better Homes and Gardens* and on various local and national radio programing, Goode has shared her holistic approach to achieving parenting success and managing family relationships. Goode holds the titles of National Certified Counselor and Diplomat of the American Psychotherapy Association. She is also the author of a dozen books, including *Help Kids Cope with Stress and Trauma, The Art and Science of Coaching Parents,* and the award-winning *Raising Intuitive Children.* She and her husband Tom Goode, ND live in Texas.

www.kidswhoseeghosts.com

To Our Readers

Weiser Books, an imprint of Red Wheel/Weiser, publishes books across the entire spectrum of occult and esoteric subjects. Our mission is to publish quality books that will make a difference in people's lives without advocating any one particular path or field of study. We value the integrity, originality, and depth of knowledge of our authors.

Our readers are our most important resource, and we appreciate your input, suggestions, and ideas about what you would like to see published. Please feel free to contact us to request our latest book catalog, or to be added to our mailing list.

Red Wheel/Weiser, LLC
500 Third Street, Suite 230
San Francisco, CA 94107
www.redwheelweiser.com